cook's essentials™

step-by-step pressure cooking cookbook

AF361145

Table of Contents

Table of Contents

BOB WARDEN'S INTRODUCTION

Congratulations on your purchase of the Cook's Essentials Pressure Cooker Cookbook. This book, like Cook's Essentials cookware and bakeware, was created at your request. Thanks to your suggestions, ideas and loyalty, over eight million pieces of cook's essentials cookware are being used in your kitchens. You have helped make Cook's Essentials stainless steel the best selling brand of stainless non-stick cookware in America!

Cook's Essential hard-coat-enamel and hard-anodized lines are widely recognized as the finest value for their cost in the world. We have enjoyed tremendous success with our cook's essentials bakeware as well; it is only a year old and already has over one million pieces in use. But no Cook's Essentials product has been more in demand that our modern pressure cookers.

As Cook's Essentials has grown, you have told us in phone calls, faxes, and emails how much fun it is to cook with the Cook's Essentials pressure cooker! You have also asked for a new cookbook designed and written especially for pressure-cooking with the modern Cook's Essentials pressure cookers. We have listened to your requests, and we expect this cookbook will exceed your expectations.

For those of you getting started for the first time or getting reacquainted to pressure-cooking, we have included an introduction to pressure-cooking. This introduction is designed to familiarize you with the basics of contemporary pressure-cooking. It will help make your pressure-cooking fast and easy. By the time you read this section, you should be well on your way to pressure-cooking success.

As I grew up on our farm in Iowa, my mother used her pressure cooker almost every day. I became accustomed to tasting the complex, infused flavors that came out of her old fashioned cooker. When I started cooking on my own, one of my first purchases was a pressure cooker. Through this book Meredith Laurence and I are happy to share with you some of our family's favorite recipes, all adapted for the Cook's Essential's pressure cooker. All of these recipes are quick, easy and delicious. Because pressure cookers are known for making some of the best comfort food ever, we have started with classic recipes for soups and stews. In addition, meats, poultry, seafood and vegetables all get their own special section. Some of my favorite one-pot meals with great infused flavors, like beef stew and barbeque spare ribs are included here. As you sample these recipes, I know you will come to appreciate and enjoy the ease and simplicity of use as well as the great tastes that are produced by pressure-cooking. You will also discover that beans and grains are now quick and easy to prepare, and that they are great as side dishes but can become complete meals when combined with other vegetable or meats. Of course, no pressure cooker cookbook would be complete without a section dedicated to desserts. If you have never made Creamy Rice Pudding or Heavenly Flan, this cookbook shows you how easy it can be with a Cook's Essentials pressure cooker.

Have fun with this book, and give us a call from time to time to tell us how you're cooking.

Enjoy!

Bob Warden and Meredith Laurence
Pressure Cooker Basics

THE BENEFITS OF PRESSURE COOKING

If you are looking for a piece of cookware that's fast, easy and healthy, nothing can quite compare to a pressure cooker. With a pressure cooker, you can save up to 70% in cooking time. And because foods cook at a much faster rate, a pressure cooker means less energy is needed and less heat is generated- a definite plus during hot weather! Another advantage to using a pressure cooker is the nutritional value. Because pressure-cooked foods require less liquid, water soluble vitamins and minerals usually evaporated by traditional cooking methods are retained in a pressure cooker. What's more, vegetables retain their vibrant colors.

Not only are Cook's Essentials pressure cookers fast, easy and healthy, they are also extremely safe. Every model has a built in safety feature with a triple-lock safety system that includes a dual pressure valve, two independent over-pressure release valves and a safety locking handle, to prevent opening under pressure.

HOW A PRESSURE COOKER WORKS

When the lid on your pressure cooker is properly locked into place, an airtight seal is created to suppress the steam created when food is heated inside the unit. At sea level, boiling water in a traditional pot reaches a maximum of 212 degrees Fahrenheit. Even if the pot is covered, steam will continue to escape and keep the temperature steady.

Because an airtight seal is created in the pressure cooker, the steam has nowhere to go and is trapped inside the pot. This causes the temperature to rise above the standard boiling temperature.

In this recipe book most recipes call for either a high pressure setting (15 psi), or low pressure (8.5 psi) setting. Choose the correct pressure setting by simply turning the dual pressure valve to the selected position.

BEFORE YOU BEGIN PRESSURE COOKING

To ensure everything is in proper working order, it is very important to check over your cooker before each use.
- Make sure the pressure cooker is clean inside and out.
  There should be no residue or food on the pot or the lid. Make sure the inner part of the lid rim, the outer rim on the pot and the rubber gasket are clean. Using a clean pressure cooker reduces the risk of the lid sticking when you open your cooker.

- Remove the rubber gasket to make sure it is pliable and is not dried out. Check for any cracks or tears. If the rubber gasket shows any sign of damage, do not use the pressure cooker. Replace the gasket immediately by contacting customer service. The number can be found at the end of this book.

- Check the safety valves. Press or gently pull on the valve to make sure it moves without any resistance. Make sure the valves are free and clear of any food particles.

LOADING THE PRESSURE COOKER

Because a pressure cooker needs space for steam to be created it is very important to never fill the cooker more than two thirds of the way full.

When preparing meat or poultry for cooking under pressure, brown them without the lid in the pressure cooker. By doing so, you will be adding flavor and extra color to the dish. In order to sear the surface of the food, make sure your stove is on medium high heat. Marinated foods should be well drained. All meat and poultry should be patted before browning.

When steaming foods, lightly coat your steaming basket with vegetable oil to prevent sticking. When steaming is done, remove the food from the steaming basket immediately.

Your Cook's Essentials pressure cooker is not a deep fryer and should never be used as one, regardless of whether the lid is on or off.

CLOSING THE COOKER

Once all the ingredients are in the pressure cooker, you have to close the lid in order to begin cooking. The Cook's Essentials pressure cookers come with an easy way to remember how to properly close the cooker. All you need to do is align the mark on the lid to the mark on the handle and gently push the base handle and upper handle together. You should never have to force your cooker closed. If there is any resistance, remove the lid and begin again.

BUILDING AND ADJUSTING PRESSURE

To build pressure inside a pressure cooker, the cooking liquid must be brought to a boil with the lid closed and locked. When the liquid boils, steam is produced and pressure is created.

Every recipe in this book calls for you to bring your cooker up to pressure. In order to do this, you must first close and lock the pressure cooker. (For safety reasons, your cooker will not come up to pressure if it is not locked.) Turn your stove to high* and wait for the pressure indicator to pop up. As soon as you begin to see a small amount of steam coming out of the pressure valve, you know your cooker is up to pressure.

Once the cooker is up to pressure, lower the heat on your stove to medium low to maintain pressure. Be careful not to lower the heat too much, otherwise you will lose pressure in your cooker and the pressure indicator will go down.

*NOTE TO ELECTRIC STOVE USERS

Since the coils on an electric stove retain heat longer than a gas stove, you will have to compensate for this. On a burner set for medium heat, bring your pressure cooker up to pressure, then lower the heat and begin cooking time. By setting the burner on medium, it will take less time for the electric coils to cool down on the burner.

TIMING YOUR RECIPES

Because the amount of time you cook foods is important to achieving the best results, we recommend you have a kitchen timer on hand.

Once the desired level of cooking pressure has been reached, set your timer for the indicated cooking time, lower your burner and begin your cooking time.

Because overcooked food cannot be corrected, it is better to cook unfamiliar foods for a shorter period of timer until you become familiar with it. You can always go back and cook foods a little longer until the desired result is reached. You will also note that some recipes have various ingredients that are added at different stages of the cooking process. It is recommended that you first add the ingredients that require more time to cook, release the pressure, add the remaining ingredients and bring up to pressure again.

RELEASING THE PRESSURE

When the food has finished cooking, remove the pressure cooker from the heat source. Although you are no longer cooking, the inside of the cooker is still very hot and the food will continue to cook. In order to stop the cooking process right away, you will have to release the pressure. This can be done in one of three ways.

NATURAL RELEASE METHOD: Foods like stock, tomato sauces and certain cuts of meat can benefit from continued cooking after the burner has been turned off. With the natural release method, the pressure will drop naturally after the unit is removed from the burner. The natural release method can take anywhere from ten to twenty minutes, depending on the kind of food you are cooking. The pressure indicator will go down once all pressure has been dissipated.

AUTOMATIC RELEASE METHOD: All Cook's Essentials models come with a spring valve mechanism in a dial format that features an automatic release setting. This can be used for releasing pressure when cooking foods such as stews, meats, poultry and soups. To use this method, turn the dial to the steam release position and wait for the pressure indicator to go down.

COLD-WATER RELEASE METHOD: Pressure is released the fastest when using this method. Take the pressure cooker over to the sink, holding both handles. Place the cooker in the sink and tilt it slightly down. Turn on the cold water and run it over the cooker until the pressure dissipates. Water should never come in contact with the upper handle of the cooker.

CARE AND MAINTENEANCE OF YOUR COOKER

As your Cook's Essentials pressure cooker is constructed of 18/10 stainless steel with a beautiful mirror finish on the exterior, it should be cleaned and maintained like any other piece of quality cookware.

After each use, wash the inside and outside of the pot and lid with mild dish soap and a non-abrasive sponge. Never immerse the lid in water, since it may affect and damage safety valves. Never wash the lid or rubber gasket in the dishwasher as this could damage the parts and dry out the gasket.

To maintain the life of your gasket, wash it with water and mild dish liquid. Massage a small amount of vegetable oil on the gasket after each use to keep it pliable.

When storing your pressure cooker, never lock the lid in place, as moisture can develop inside the cooker and damage your gasket. Always store the lid in the upside down position.

ELECTRIC PRESSURE COOKER MODELS

All of the recipes in this cookbook are suitable for not only stovetop pressure cookers, but electric pressure cookers as well. Electric Pressure cookers function in the same fashion as stovetop pressure cookers. To make following the recipes in this book a little easier when using electric models, please read the following operational tips.

- Use the "Brown" function on the electric pressure cookers to sear, sauté or brown foods before cooking them under pressure. This simulates cooking foods on a stovetop burner over medium high heat. Use this function without the lid on the unit.

- Use the "Steam" function on the electric pressure cookers to steam or boil foods. This mode will bring water to a boil, as though on a stovetop burner over high heat. When using "Steam", place the lid on the pressure cooker and set the pressure regulator knob on the lid to "Steam".

- The "Warm" mode on an electric pressure cooker will re-heat foods or keep food warm for an indefinite period of time. This feature can also be used in conjunction with the other cooking modes, programming the pressure cooker to keep food warm after cooking it.

- Remember to always set the pressure regulator knob to "Pressure" when using the electric pressure cooker in low or high-pressure mode.

- Electric pressure cookers do require that you program a certain amount of time for the cooking mode. Set the time for the amount of time suggested in the recipe. The timer will only begin to count down once the proper pressure has been reached inside the cooker.

Soups & Stocks
& Sauces

BEEF STOCK

This recipe for beef stock will beat any canned variety you may find at the local supermarket. You can prepare this stock ahead of time and store it in your freezer for up to six months.

Serves 6

Ingredients

1 tablespoon olive oil
2 pounds stewing beef; such as shanks, cut in 1" cubes
1 pound beef bones
8 cups water
1 medium onion, coarsely chopped
1 large carrot, scraped and coarsely chopped
1 bay leaf
Salt to taste*
6 peppercorns
1 celery stalk, coarsely chopped
2 sprigs parsley
1/2 teaspoon thyme

Directions

Heat the olive oil in the cooker until very hot. Add beef and bones, as much as will comfortably fit at once. Cook until well browned. Repeat with remaining beef and bones until all meat is browned. Drain away any excess fat.

Add all remaining ingredients, close lid and bring to high pressure. Once pressure has been reached, lower the heat and cook for 1 hour. Release pressure using the automatic release method and remove the lid.

Strain the stock through a colander, pressing with the back of a wooden spoon to extract as much liquid as possible. Refrigerate overnight and skim away any fat from the surface.

Approximate Nutritional Information Per Serving

60 calories, 7g protein, 3g carbohydrates, 2.5g fat, 0mg cholesterol, 110mg sodium
*not included nutritional analysis

Estimated Prep Time: . . . .*10 minutes*
Estimated Cooking Time: . . . .*1 hour*
Total: *1h 10minutes*

CHICKEN STOCK

Having homemade chicken stock around the house comes in handy very often. It can be used as the base for many types of gravy, and of course, hundreds of soups. Chicken backs or wings tend to work best when making this stock.

Serves 6

Ingredients

2 pounds chicken parts, primarily backs, but also including gizzards, necks, hearts and wings
1 medium onion, peeled and halved
1 celery stalk, cut in several pieces
1 large carrot, scraped and cut in several pieces
2 sprigs parsley
6 peppercorns
1 teaspoon thyme 1 bay leaf
6 cups water
Salt to taste*

Directions

Combine all ingredients in the pressure cooker. Close the lid and bring to high pressure. Once high pressure has been reached, lower the heat and cook for 30 minutes. Release pressure using the automatic release method and remove the lid.

Strain the stock through a colander, pressing with the back of a wooden spoon to extract as much liquid as possible. Refrigerate overnight and skim away any fat from the surface.

Approximate Nutritional Information Per Serving

45 calories, 6g protein, 3g carbohydrates, 0g fat, 0mg cholesterol, 180mg sodium
*not included in nutritional analysis

Estimated Prep Time: . . . .*7 minutes*
Estimated Cooking Time: . . . .*30 minutes*
Total: . . . .*37 minutes*

FISH STOCK

When making this stock, pour a small amount of oil on top before closing the lid. This will help inhibit foaming during cooking. Be sure to use this stock within two months, as fish is more delicate and spoils faster than chicken or beef.

(Serves 6)

Ingredients

2 pounds fish and shellfish meat, bones, heads and shells
1 celery stalk, cut in several pieces
1 carrot, cut in several pieces
1 bay leaf
1 teaspoon thyme
4 peppercorns
2 sprigs parsley 1 bay leaf
1 onion, peeled and sliced
6 cups water
1/2 teaspoon olive oil
Salt to taste*

Directions

Combine all ingredients in the pressure cooker. Close the lid and bring to high pressure. Once high pressure has been reached, lower the heat and cook for 25 minutes. Release pressure using the automatic release method and remove the lid.

Strain the stock through a colander, pressing with the back of a wooden spoon to extract as much liquid as possible. Refrigerate overnight and skim away any fat from the surface.

Approximate Nutritional Information Per Serving

25 calories, 1g protein, 5g carbohydrates, 0g fat, 5mg cholesterol, 90 mg sodium
*not included in nutritional analysis

Estimated Prep Time: . . . .*5 minutes*
Estimated Cooking Time: . . . .*25 minutes*
Total: . . . .*30 minutes*

VEGETABLE STOCK

Even meat lovers can appreciate homemade vegetable stock. Delicious as an addition to a recipe or on its own, vegetable stock is truly versatile. In many recipes, chicken or beef stock is easily replaced with vegetable stock.

(Serves 6)

Ingredients

2 tablespoons olive or vegetable oil
1 large potato, scrubbed and cut into 2" pieces
3 medium celery stalks with leaves, chopped
3 medium carrots, chopped
2 medium onions, chopped
1 whole head of garlic
6 parsley sprigs
1 teaspoon salt

Directions

Heat oil over medium heat and add potato, celery, carrots, onions, and garlic. Cook until onions are translucent.

Fill cooker halfway with water and stir in parsley, bay leaf and salt. Close lid, bring to high pressure and cook for 20 minutes. Release pressure using the cold water release method.

Strain stock through a colander and cool completely. Skim off excess fat off top.

Approximate Nutritional Information Per Serving

50 calories, 0g protein, 3g carbohydrates, 4.5g fat, 0mg cholesterol, 400mg sodium

Estimated Prep Time: . . . .*7 minutes*
Estimated Cooking Time: . . . .*20 minutes*
Total: . . . .*27 minutes*

QUICK & EASY CHICKEN SOUP

Forget spending hours making homemade chicken soup. The pressure cooker will soon become your best friend in the kitchen after you taste this excellent recipe for homemade chicken soup. And it only takes 12 minutes!

(Serves 8)

Ingredients

    5 pound chicken, cut up
    8 cups water
    2 medium onions, peeled and quartered
    1 carrot, chopped
    1 parsnip, chopped
    1 celery stalk, chopped
    1 bay leaf
    1 teaspoon dried thyme
    a few sprigs fresh parsley
    8 whole black peppercorns
    1 1/2 tsp. Salt
    1/3 cup uncooked rice or noodles

Directions

Combine all the ingredients with the water and add to pressure cooker. Close lid bring to high pressure and cook for 12 minutes. Release pressure using the automatic release method. Open cooker and discard the fat that rises to the surface (the best way to remove the fat is to chill the stock overnight. The fat will harden on top that makes it easy to scoop off).

Stir. Meat will fall off bones. Remove bones and fat. Return the stock to the cleaned pressure cooker and simmer until reduced by half. Add salt to taste. Add rice or noodles to stock until cooked through. Enjoy straight up with saltine crackers.

Approximate Nutritional Information Per Serving

300 calories, 51g protein, 9g carbohydrates, 6g fat, 130mg cholesterol, 200mg sodium

    Estimated Prep Time: . . . .*10 minutes*
    Estimated Cooking Time: . . . .*12 minutes*
    Total: . . . .*22 minutes*

RUDDY ONION SOUP

A traditional Parisian soup, this Americanized version of the recipe is truly delicious. Serve the soup very hot with shredded cheeses and toasted bread on the side.

(Serves 4)

Ingredients

    1 tablespoon olive oil
    1 tablespoon flour
    7 cups yellow onions, julienne style
    2 teaspoons garlic, minced
    2 cups vegetable stock or water
    1/2 cup dry sherry
    1/2 cup dry vermouth
    2 tablespoons tomato sauce
    2 tablespoons soy sauce
    1/4 cup scallion tops, minced
    Salt and pepper to taste*

Directions

In pressure cooker over medium heat, add the olive oil and flour. Stir to form a paste. Cook paste mixture until it turns a light brown color, approximately 3-5 minutes. Add the onions and garlic to the paste mixture and sauté for 5 minutes, stirring continuously, until the onion begin to soften. Add the stock or water, wine and tomato sauce to the pressure cooker.

Close the lid and bring to high pressure. Once high pressure has been reached, lower the heat and cook for 4 minutes. Release pressure using cold-water release method and open the cooker. Season with soy sauce and add the scallion tops. Taste and adjust the seasoning with salt and pepper if needed. For a thinner soup, add more stock or water.

Approximate Nutritional Information Per Serving

220 calories, 5g protein, 31g carbohydrates, 4g fat, 0mg cholesterol, 710mg sodium
*not included in nutritional analysis

    Estimated Prep Time: . . . .*10 minutes*
    Estimated Cooking Time: . . . .*13 minutes*
    Total: . . . .*23 minutes*

GREEN SPLIT PEA WITH HAM

This is truly a classic recipe. Many may remember their grandmothers used to make this soup on Sunday afternoons. They would spend hours simmering that big pot to get the flavor of ham "just right." The pressure cooker version only takes 10 minutes!

(Serves 8)

Ingredients

1 pound green split peas
2 large smoked ham hocks, about 1-1/2 pounds total
1 large onion, chopped
1 stalk celery, chopped
1 large carrot, chopped
10 sprigs parsley
4 sprigs fresh thyme
1 bay leaf
8 cups cold water
1 1/4 teaspoon kosher salt
Freshly ground black pepper, to taste*

Directions

Combine the peas, hocks, onion, celery and carrot in the pressure cooker. Tie the parsley, thyme, and bay leaf together with kitchen string and add the herb bundle, water, and salt. Close the lid, bring to high pressure and cook for 10 minutes. Release pressure using the automatic release method and remove the lid. Cool the soup for at least 20 minutes. Remove and discard the herb bundle and take the hocks out of the pressure cooker. Remove all meat from the hocks and discard the bones, fat and skin. Cut the meat into cubes. Puree the soup with a hand held blender or in batches in a traditional blender. Once all soup is pureed, add the mixture back to the pressure cooker and bring to a simmer. Taste and adjust seasoning by adding salt and pepper to taste. Serve in heated bowls with croutons, if desired.

Approximate Nutritional Information Per Serving

360 calories, 27g protein, 33g carbohydrates, 13g fat, 60mg cholesterol, 480mg sodium
*not included in nutritional analysis

Estimated Prep Time: . . . . .5 minutes
Estimated Cooking Time: . . . . .35 minutes
Total: .40 minutes

MANHATTAN CLAM CHOWDER

A hint of spice in the red broth combined with colorful chunks of green peppers, celery and tomatoes; the pressure cooker version of the classic soup makes you feel like you are sitting in a café in Soho.

(Serves 4)

Ingredients

4 slices bacon, diced
1 medium onion, finely chopped
1 clove garlic, minced
1/4 cup diced green pepper
1 tablespoon flour
1 large potato, diced
1/4 cup finely chopped celery
14 ounce can whole tomatoes, chopped
2 1/2 cups clam juice, fish stock, or water
1 bay leaf
Freshly ground pepper, to taste
1 cup minced clams, preferably fresh

Directions

Add the bacon to the pressure cooker and sauté. Once all fat has been rendered, add the onion, garlic and green pepper and cook until the green pepper is softened. Stir in the flour and then add the potato, celery, tomato, clam juice, bay leaf and pepper.

Close lid, bring to high pressure, lower heat and cook for 5 minutes. Release pressure using the automatic release method and open cooker. Discard the bay leaf. Stir in the clams and serve.

Note: The soup gains flavor if it sits a few hours at room temperature or is refrigerated overnight.

Approximate Nutritional Information Per Serving

270 calories, 15 g protein, 19g carbohydrates, 15g fat, 35mg cholesterol, 580mg sodium

Estimated Prep Time: . . . . .10 minutes
Estimated Cooking Time: . . . . .10 minutes
Total: .20 minutes

MINESTRONE

Minestrone soup is never made the same way twice. The recipe that follows can be used as a guideline for your own imaginative additions (or omissions). Use vegetables that are in season for truly original combinations.

(Serves 4)

Ingredients

1/3 cup olive oil
1 cup chopped onion
1 cup diced celery
1 cup diced carrots
1/2 cup great northern beans, soaked
1 bay leaf
Sprig of thyme
2 cups diced potatoes
2 cups zucchini, diced, about 2 small zucchini
2 cups shredded savoy cabbage
Rind of a piece of Parmesan cheese-optional*
2 cups Italian canned tomatoes and their juice
4 cups beef stock
Salt and pepper to taste*
1 cup small pasta shells

Directions

Heat olive oil in the pressure cooker and add onions. Cook until golden, about 5 to 7 minutes. Then, add celery and carrots and cook over low heat, stirring occasionally, for 5 minutes. Add beans, bay leaf, thyme and toss for 1 minute. Add potatoes, zucchini, savoy cabbage, and stir. Add the Parmesan rind (if using), plum tomatoes and their juice, beef stock, and salt and pepper to taste. Close lid, bring to high pressure and cook for 10 minutes. Release pressure using the cold-water release method. Finally, add your pasta and cook, covered for about 10 minutes. Season again with salt and pepper and ladle into bowls.

Approximate Nutritional Information Per Serving

530 calories, 18g protein, 70g carbohydrates, 21g fat, 0mg cholesterol, 300mg sodium

Estimated Prep Time: . . . . .10 minutes
Estimated Cooking Time: . . . . .30 minutes
Total: . . . . .40 minutes

TRADITIONAL MARINARA SAUCE

We all know that making a great marinara sauce calls for simmering and stirring for hours on end. By using the pressure cooker, the flavors are intensified and the end result is a delicious, rich tasting sauce.

(Serves 8)

Ingredients

3 tablespoons olive oil
1/2 cup onion, minced
2 garlic cloves, minced
1 tablespoon tomato paste
2 28-ounce cans tomatoes, Italian-style, reserving juice from one can
2 teaspoons dried oregano
2 teaspoons dried basil
1/2 teaspoon sugar
1/4 cup fresh parsley, minced
Salt and pepper, to taste*

Directions

Add the olive oil to the pressure cooker and heat over medium heat. Add onion and garlic and sauté for approximately 2 minutes. Do not brown onion. Add tomato paste and reserved tomato juice. Cook for 2 minutes longer, stirring constantly. Add tomatoes, oregano, basil, and sugar. Gently break up tomatoes against side of pot as you cook.

Close the lid, bring to high pressure, then lower heat and cook for 20 minutes. Release pressure using the automatic release method and open lid.

Season to taste with salt and pepper. Just before serving, stir parsley into sauce. Serve with your favorite pasta.

Approximate Nutritional Information Per Serving

100 calories, 2g protein, 9g carbohydrates, 5g fat, 0mg cholesterol, 360mg sodium
*not included in nutritional analysis

Estimated Prep Time: . . . . .5 minutes
Estimated Cooking Time: . . . . .24 minutes
Total: . . . . .29 minutes

CLASSIC BOLOGNESE SAUCE

An excellent chunky pasta sauce with beef, lots of vegetables and tons of flavor. Freeze any unused portions for later use. If you have fresh herbs, you may substitute 2 teaspoons chopped fresh basil for the dried basil in this recipe.

(Serves 8)

Ingredients

2 tablespoons olive oil
1 tablespoons unsalted butter
1/4 cup minced pancetta
2/3 cup minced carrot
1 cup minced celery
1/2 cup minced onion
1 lb ground beef chuck
salt & freshly ground pepper to taste

1 cup milk
1/2 cup dry white wine
3 cups canned plum tomatoes, chopped with liquid
1/2 teaspoon dried basil
1 lb pasta*
freshly grated Parmesan cheese- optional garnish*

Directions

In pressure cooker, heat oil and butter. Add pancetta and cook for 6 to 8 minutes, or until most of the fat has been rendered. Then add carrots, celery, and onions and sauté for 3 minutes. Add the beef and cook until the beef is no longer pink. Add the milk and simmer gently, stirring occasionally, until the milk is completely evaporated. Add wine and simmer until evaporated. Finally, add the tomatoes and basil and salt and pepper to taste.

Close lid and bring to high pressure. Cook at high pressure for 15 minutes. Release pressure using the natural release method. When almost ready to serve, bring a large pot of salted water to a boil. Cook the pasta until it is tender but still firm to the bite, 10 to 12 minutes. Drain, and return to the pot. Add sauce to the pasta and toss to combine. Transfer to a serving bowl, and serve immediately. Top with freshly grated Parmesan cheese if desired.

Approximate Nutritional Information Per Serving

178 calories, 14g protein, 6g carbohydrates, 10g fat, 35mg cholesterol, 190mg sodium
*not included in nutritional analysis

Estimated Prep Time: . . . . .10 minutes
Estimated Cooking Time: . . . . .25 minutes
Total: . . . . .35 minutes

SWEET & SOUR CABBAGE SOUP

Several years ago a cabbage soup diet fad spread nationwide proclaimed that eating this soup would everyday would dramatically decrease your waistline. While we make no promises of any weight loss from eating this soup, it sure does taste great!

(Serves 6)

Ingredients

3 tablespoons olive oil
1 large onion, chopped
2 garlic cloves, minced
1 teaspoon crushed red pepper flakes
_ cup balsamic vinegar
2 tablespoons brown sugar
6 cups finely sliced red cabbage
1 cup chopped and drained plum tomatoes
6 cups chicken stock
1/4 tsp. salt and pepper
_ cup finely chopped fresh parsley
Sour cream and finely chopped fresh chives, as accompaniments*

Directions

Heat olive oil in pressure cooker and cook onions until translucent. Add minced garlic, red pepper flakes and cook for one minute. Stir in balsamic vinegar, brown sugar, cabbage, tomatoes, and chicken stock.

Close the lid and bring to high pressure. Once high pressure is reached, lower heat and cook for 12 minutes. Release pressure using the automatic release method and open cooker.

Taste soup and adjust seasoning with more balsamic vinegar, brown sugar, salt and/or pepper, if desired. Stir in parsley. Serve hot with a dollop of sour cream and chives.

Approximate Nutritional Information Per Serving

170 calories, 5g protein, 15g carbohydrates, 12g fat, 10mg cholesterol, 350mg sodium
*not included in nutritional analysis

Estimated Prep Time: . . . . .5 minutes
Estimated Cooking Time: . . . . .15 minutes
Total: . . . . .20 minutes

Meats & Poultry

COOKING TIMES FOR MEATS & POULTRY

- **Always cook meat or poultry with at least 1/2 cup of liquid. If the cooking time exceeds 15 minutes, use 2 cups of liquid.**

- **Preserved or salted meats should be covered (immerse the meat in the water).**

- **Exact cooking times for meat and poultry vary according to the quality and quantity of meat or poultry being cooked.**

- **Unless indicated, the cooking times given below are for 3 pounds of meat or poultry. Also, the denser the cut, the longer the cooking time should be.**

APPROXIMATE COOKING MINUTES

BEEF/VEAL, ROAST OR BRISKET	35-40
BEEF MEATLOAF, 2 IBS.	10-15
BEEF, MEATBALLS, 1-2 IBS.	5-10
BEEF, CORNED	50-60
PORK, ROAST	40-45
PORK, RIBS, 2 IBS.	15
PORK, HAM SHANK	20-25
LAMB, LEG OF	35-40
CHICKEN, WHOLE, 2-3 IBS.	12-15
CHICKEN, PIECES, 2-3 IBS.	8-10
CORNISH HENS, TWO	8-10

CARIBBEAN BEEF ROAST

You'll be whisked away to a tropical location when you try this sumptuous beef roast. The citrus flavor in this dish combines perfectly with the spiciness of the peppers. For extra flavor in the meat, try marinating the roast for at least 3-4 hours in the beef bouillon, garlic powder, black pepper, nutmeg, limejuice and vinegar.

(Serves 6)

Ingredients

2 pounds lean trimmed chuck shoulder roast
1 tablespoon fresh chopped cilantro
1/4 cup chopped onion
1 teaspoon garlic powder
1/4 cup chopped celery
1/2 cup chopped green bell pepper
1 teaspoon cracked black pepper
1/4 teaspoon nutmeg
1 red jalapeno, diced
1 tablespoon fresh chopped parsley
1 tablespoon fresh chopped thyme
1 tablespoon beef bouillon granules
1 tablespoon limejuice
2 tablespoons red wine vinegar
Cooked rice with crushed pineapple*

Directions

Place the trivet and steamer basket inside the pressure cooker and add 1 1/2 cups water. Place beef in steamer basket and surround with vegetables and fresh herbs. In small bowl, combine beef bouillon granules, garlic powder, black pepper, nutmeg, limejuice and vinegar. Stir well and spoon over beef.

Close lid, bring up to high pressure, then lower heat and cook for 25 minutes. Release pressure using the automatic release method. Prepare rice while beef is cooking, adding 1 cup crushed pineapple to rice. Serve beef with vegetables and pineapple rice.

Approximate Nutritional Information Per Serving

570 calories, 72g protein, 6g carbohydrates, 27g fat, 240mg cholesterol, 430mg sodium

Estimated Prep Time: . . . .*10 minutes*
Estimated Cooking Time: . . . .*25 minutes*
Total: . . . .*35 minutes*

BARBEQUE SPARE RIBS

Try this recipe for the most tender barbeque ribs you have ever tasted! Forget boiling ribs before cooking or slow grilling them for hours, because when you use your pressure cooker you cut 70% of the usual cooking time off. The result is succulent spare ribs that taste great yet take much less time.

Serves 4

Ingredients

1 Tablespoon vegetable oil
1 medium onion, chopped
2 garlic cloves, chopped
2/3 cup prepared barbeque sauce
1/2 cup water
3 pounds pork spare ribs
1/4 teaspoon salt
1/8 teaspoon black pepper

Directions

Heat oil over medium heat in the pressure cooker and sauté onions and garlic for 2 minutes. Stir in barbeque sauce and water and simmer 5 minutes. Add spare ribs and close pressure cooker lid. Bring to high pressure and cook for 18 minutes. Release pressure using the cold water release method.

Remove ribs from the cooker and transfer to an oiled broiler rack. Season with salt and pepper. Position broiler pan 6 inches from source of heat. Broil lightly on one side and remove from oven. While ribs are broiling, boil remaining cooking liquid over medium high heat until it begins to thicken (about 5 minutes). Brush the thickened sauce over the ribs and broil for an additional 2-3 minutes. Turn over, brush sauce on and broil for 2-3 more minutes. Serve hot.

Approximate Nutritional Information Per Serving

710 calories, 48g protein, 8g carbohydrates, 53g fat, 195mg cholesterol, 640mg sodium

Estimated Prep Time: . . . .*2 minutes*
Estimated Cooking Time: . . . .*29 minutes*
Total: . . . .*31 minutes*

CORNED BEEF AND CABBAGE

Corned beef and cabbage is usually a once a year meal. It's not because you don't love the taste, it's because you just don't have the time it takes to prepare it. Using traditional cooking methods, you could easily spend 3-4 hours simmering the corned beef. This pressure cooker recipe achieves the same great flavors as traditional cooking, but only takes one hour!

Serves 6

Ingredients

2 cups water
12 ounce bottle of lager beer
2 medium onions, peeled and cut in half
2 garlic cloves
3 pound corned beef brisket with spice packet
4 medium red potatoes, cut into 1" pieces
4 medium carrots, cut into 1" pieces
1 small cabbage, cut into wedges

Directions

Add water, beer, onions, garlic, and corned beef with spice packet into pressure cooker. Close the lid and bring to high pressure. Cook for 1 hour. Release pressure using the natural release method.

Transfer meat to serving plate and cover with foil. Add 1/4 cup water or beef stock to pressure cooker to deglaze pan. Place potatoes, carrots and cabbage in the cooker. Close lid, bring to high pressure and cook for 6 minutes. Release pressure using the cold water release method.

Slice corned beef against the grain and serve with vegetables on the side.

Approximate Nutritional Information Per Serving

610 calories, 40g protein, 36g carbohydrates, 34g fat, 120mg cholesterol, 320mg sodium

Estimated Prep Time: . . . .*5 minutes*
Estimated Cooking Time: . . . .*1h 6 minutes*
Total: . . . .*1h 11 minutes*

TRADITIONAL LAMB STEW

The chilies in this dish add a bit of spice to this flavorful stew. Serve with French bread on the side for dipping.

Serves 6

Ingredients

1 cup drained del pequillo chiles or 7 oz. can serrano chiles
Olive oil, for sautéing
3 lb. piece lamb shoulder or 3 lbs. lamb shoulder chops
1 cup onions, 1/4-inch dice
4 cloves garlic, minced
1/4 pound serrano ham, sliced or 1/2 cup pancetta, minced
1 cup fino (dry) or amontillado (semi-dry) sherry
1 cup ruby port
1 cup dry white wine
14 1/2 ounce can Italian style chopped tomatoes
1 bay leaf
2 rosemary sprigs

Directions

Soak chiles in hot water for 5 minutes.

In pressure cooker heat oil and brown lamb on all sides. Remove from pot. Add onions, garlic, and ham and sauté until soft. Add del pequillo chiles and all 3 wines to deglaze pan. Stir 1-2 minutes to remove any small bits of meat or vegetables stuck to bottom of pan.

Return lamb to pot along with tomatoes, bay leaf and rosemary. Close lid, bring to high pressure and cook for 1 hour. Release pressure using the automatic release method. Remove bones before serving.

Approximate Nutritional Information Per Serving

533 calories, 33g protein, 12g carbohydrates, 28g fat, 123mg cholesterol, 660mg sodium

Estimated Prep Time: . . . .*5 minutes*
Estimated Cooking Time: . . . .*1 h 10 minutes*
Total: . . . .*1 h 15 minutes*

RICE WITH CHICKEN & CHORIZO SAUSAGE

A common dish in Hispanic households, this recipe calls for chorizo sausage, which is dried and cured. It is very flavorful and will add a distinct flavor and authentic look to this dish.

Serves 6

Ingredients

2 tablespoons olive oil
1/2 green bell pepper, chopped finely
1/2 red bell pepper, chopped finely
1/2 cup green peas, fresh or frozen
1/2 cup sweet corn, fresh or frozen
1/2 pound chicken breast, cut into small pieces
1 chorizo sausage (about 6 oz.), cut into small pieces
1 cup Spanish rice (or short-medium grain, Arborio type)
4 cups water

Directions

Heat the olive oil over medium heat in the pressure cooker and add the peppers. Sauté for 5 minutes or until they begin to soften. Add the peas and sweet corn and cook for another minute. Next, add the chicken and chorizo sausage, mix well, and sauté for 2 additional minutes. Finally, add the rice, stirring, allowing it to absorb the olive oil. Cover with 4 cups of water.

Close the lid and bring to high pressure, then lower heat and cook for 6 minutes. Release pressure using the automatic release method, remove the lid and serve.

Approximate Nutritional Information Per Serving

320 calories, 18g protein, 26g carbohydrates, 17g fat, 45mg cholesterol, 390mg sodium

Estimated Prep Time: . . . .*5 minutes*
Estimated Cooking Time: . . . .*10 minutes*
Total: . . . .*15 minutes*

TRADITIONAL BEEF STEW

Packed with vegetables, this stew is great for a hearty meal without the extra calories. To cut additional calories, be sure to trim all visible fat from the beef before browning.

Serves 8

Ingredients

2 tablespoons vegetable oil
1 cup flour
2 1/2 pounds beef chuck, cut into 2-inch cubes
Kosher salt and freshly ground black pepper
2 tablespoons unsalted butter
2 medium onions, cut into sixths
5 cloves garlic, minced
1 tablespoon tomato paste
8 cups cold water, or chicken or beef broth, homemade or low-sodium canned
6 sprigs parsley
6 sprigs fresh thyme
2 bay leaves
salt and black pepper, to taste
1-1/4 pounds medium red potatoes, quartered
4 medium carrots, cut into
    1-inch pieces
2 celery stalks, cut into 1-inch pieces
7 canned whole, peeled tomatoes, lightly crushed
1 tablespoon red wine vinegar

Directions

Heat oil in cooker until pan is hot, but not smoking. Season beef generously with salt and pepper and dredge in the flour. Shake off the excess flour. Sauté the meat in 3 separate batches, uncovered, stirring only occasionally, until well-browned. Meat should cover bottom of pot without layering to allow meat to brown. Transfer the beef to a plate. Discard the oil and wipe out the pan. Repeat with 2 remaining batches.

Return the pot to the stove and melt the butter over medium high heat. Add the onion and cook, stirring, until lightly browned, about 5 minutes. Add the garlic and cook about 1 minute. Add the tomato paste and cook, stirring, until lightly browned, about 1 minute more. Return the beef to the pot, add the water or broth, and bring to a simmer.

Using a piece of kitchen twine, tie together the parsley, thyme, and bay leaves and add the bundle to the pot. Season with 2 teaspoons salt and pepper to taste. Close lid and bring to high pressure. Cook for 30 minutes.
Release pressure and open lid. Add the potatoes, carrots, celery, and the tomatoes, and close lid. Bring to high pressure and cook for 6 minutes. Release pressure and remove and discard the herb bundle. Stir in the vinegar and season with salt and pepper to taste. Divide among bowls and serve immediately.

Approximate Nutritional Information Per Serving

562 calories, 32g protein, 38g carbohydrates, 32g fat, 105mg cholesterol, 240mg sodium

Estimated Prep Time: . . . . .10 minutes
Estimated Cooking Time: . . . . .46 minutes
Total: . . . . .56 minutes

CITRUS CHICKEN

If you're tired of the same old chicken, this dish will wake up your taste buds. The unusual combination of citrus flavors coupled with honey and spices blend excellently with the natural flavor of the chicken.

Serves 6

Ingredients

1-4 lb. chicken
1/3 cup orange juice
1/4 cup frozen lemon juice concentrate, thawed
1/8 teaspoon salt
1/8 teaspoon pepper
1/4 cup honey
3 tablespoons chopped mint leaves
1/4 cup olive oil
1/4 teaspoon cumin
3 tablespoon fresh lime juice
Pinch of thyme
1/4 cup fresh lemon juice
1/4 teaspoon cinnamon
1 teaspoon grated orange peel
1 onion, sliced
2 teaspoons grated lemon peel
1 can low sodium chicken broth
I teaspoon grated lime peel
I cup of water

Directions

Wash chicken and set aside. In large bowl, combine all ingredients except onion, broth and water. Mix well. Add chicken to mixture, turning a few times to cover with marinade. Slice onion and toss in bowl. Cover bowl with aluminum foil. Marinate 3-8 hours. When ready to cook, place chicken in pressure cooker. Add marinade, chicken broth and water. Place lid on cooker, bring up to high pressure, then lower heat and cook for 25 minutes. Release pressure using the automatic release method, open lid and serve with steamed vegetables.

Approximate Nutritional Information Per Serving

400 calories, 35g protein, 16g carbohydrates, 22g fat, 110mg cholesterol, 170mg sodium

Estimated Prep Time: . . . .*5 minutes*
Estimated Cooking Time: . . . .*25 minutes*
Total: . . . .*30 minutes*

SPANISH GOLD SAUTÉED CHICKEN

Full of taste and aroma, the robust ingredients in this dish blend together to create a flavor that is piquant, yet not overpowering. Serve over white rice to balance the flavors.

Serves 4

Ingredients

1 tablespoon olive oil
1 cup orange Juice
1/2 teaspoon each: salt, lemon pepper
   seasoning, ground cumin
1/2 cup Rioja or other dry red wine
1/2 cup low sodium chicken broth
4 boneless chicken breast halves
2 tablespoons honey
1 medium leek, white part only,
   chopped
1 large plum tomato, seeded, diced
2 garlic cloves, minced
3 cups hot cooked rice
3 lemon slices, 1/4-inch thick
1/4 cup chopped fresh parsley
I 1/2 cup pitted prunes
Lemon slices, for garnish
1/3 cup pitted green olives, cut in half
2 tablespoons minced fresh or 2
   teaspoons dried thyme

Directions

Heat olive oil in the pressure cooker over high heat. Combine salt, lemon pepper seasoning and cumin sprinkle over both sides of chicken breasts.

Add chicken to pressure cooker and sauté on both sides, about 5 minutes. Transfer chicken to plate and keep warm. Reduce heat to medium-high. Add leek and garlic, cook and stir about 3 minutes. Add chicken, lemon slices, prunes, olives and thyme. Combine orange juice, wine, chicken broth and honey; pour over chicken. Close lid, bring to high pressure, then lower heat and cook for 25 minutes. Remove from heat and release the pressure with the cold-water release method. Remove lid, set cooker back on stove and stir in tomatoes. Turn heat on low and cook for approximately 2 more minutes, stirring frequently.

Serve chicken mixture over rice. Sprinkle with parsley. Garnish with lemon slices.

Approximate Nutritional Information Per Serving

530 calories, 40g protein, 70g carbohydrates, 9g fat, 95mg cholesterol, 450mg sodium

Estimated Prep Time: . . . .*10 minutes*
Estimated Cooking Time: . . . .*35 minutes*
Total: . . . .*45 minutes*

ACAPULCO CHICKEN

Not your everyday chicken recipe, this dish was inspired by the distinctive and appetizing flavor combinations of the Caribbean. Serve over white or brown rice.

Serves 4

Ingredients

3 thick whole boneless chicken breasts, cut into 1" chunks
1/4 Cup olive oil
3 tablespoons brown sugar
1 teaspoon cinnamon
1/2 teaspoon grated ginger
1 1/2 cups orange juice
1 cup rice
1/2 cup raisins
1/2 cup orange marmalade
1/2 cup flaked coconut
Salt and pepper to taste*

Directions

In saucepan, heat orange juice, raisins and marmalade and stir until marmalade melts. Remove from heat and set aside.

Heat olive oil in pressure cooker and add chicken chunks. Lightly brown. Add the orange juice mixture plus the brown sugar, cinnamon, ginger and rice.

Close lid and bring to high pressure, then lower heat and cook for 10 minutes. Remove from heat and release using the cold-water release. Open, stir, taste and add salt and pepper to taste.

To serve, place chicken and rice on dish and sprinkle with flaked coconut.

Approximate Nutritional Information Per Serving

770 calories, 46g protein, 105g carbohydrates, 19g fat, 105mg cholesterol, 170mg sodium
*not included in nutritional analysis

Estimated Prep Time: . . . . .5 minutes
Estimated Cooking Time: . . . . .15 minutes
Total: . . . . .20 minutes

CHICKEN ADOBO

Easy, fast and tasty, this is a traditional meal from the islands of Hawaii.

Serves 4

Ingredients

1 1/2 pounds chicken drumsticks
2 cups vinegar
1 1/2 cups low sodium soy sauce
1/4 cup water
2 Bay leaves
Peppercorn, to taste
3 cloves garlic, crushed
1 large red onion, chopped
3 Tbsp oil

Directions

Heat oil in pressure cooker and brown chicken on all sides. Once chicken is browned, add onion and garlic and sauté until soft.

Add all remaining ingredients to the cooker and stir. Close pressure cooker lid, bring to high pressure and cook for 30 minutes. Release pressure using the cold water release method.

Serve over rice.

Approximate Nutritional Information Per Serving

370 calories, 27g protein, 28g carbohydrates, 19g fat, 70mg cholesterol, 3260mg sodium

Estimated Prep Time: . . . . .5 minutes
Estimated Cooking Time: . . . . .35 minutes
Total: . . . . .40 minutes

BARBEQUE CHICKEN

Even in a snowstorm, you can enjoy barbecued chicken when it comes from a pressure cooker.

Serves 4

Ingredients

1 Tablespoon vegetable oil
1 medium onion
2 garlic cloves, chopped
2/3 cup prepared barbeque sauce
1/2 cup water
One small chicken, quartered
1/4 teaspoon salt
1/8 teaspoon black pepper

Directions

Heat oil in the pressure cooker and sauté onions and garlic for 2 minutes. Stir in barbeque sauce and water. Simmer 5 minutes to slightly thicken.

Add chicken pieces and close pressure cooker lid. Bring to high pressure and cook for 10 minutes. Release pressure using the cold water release method.

Remove chicken from the cooker and transfer to an oiled broiler rack. Season with salt and pepper. Position broiler pan 6 inches from source of heat.

Boil remaining cooking liquid until it begins to thicken (about 5 minutes). Brush the thickened sauce over the chicken and broil for 2-3 minutes.

Approximate Nutritional Information Per Serving

610 calories, 59g protein, 8g carbohydrates, 36g fat, 180mg cholesterol, 660mg sodium

Estimated Prep Time: . . . . .2 minutes
Estimated Cooking Time: . . . . .20 minutes
Total: . . . . .22 minutes

TURKEY CHILI

Try this recipe for a great alternative to traditional ground beef chili. Using turkey as a replacement for ground beef tastes great and also reduces fat and calories by up to 50%.

Serves 6

Ingredients

1/4 cup olive oil
1 onion, finely sliced
2 garlic cloves, minced or crushed
2 tablespoons chili powder
2 teaspoons ground cumin powder
1/2 teaspoon ground cinnamon
2 tablespoons cider vinegar
28-ounce can plum tomatoes, drained and chopped
16 to 19-ounce can kidney beans, drained and rinsed
1 pound boneless skinless turkey breast, cut into 3/4-inch cubes
Garnish - sour cream, seeded red bell pepper cut into 1/2 inch dice; cilantro leaves, coarsely chopped*
About 12 corn tortillas*

Directions

Heat olive oil in pressure cooker. When hot, add onion and sauté for 5 minutes or until tender. Add garlic, chili, cumin and cinnamon and sauté for 60 seconds. Add cider vinegar and cook 1 minute to deglaze pan. Add tomatoes, and simmer uncovered for 5 minutes.

Add beans and turkey. Close lid, bring to high pressure and cook for 5 minutes. Release pressure using the cold water release method.

Serve with corn tortillas (or rice).

Approximate Nutritional Information Per Serving

300 calories, 26g protein, 26g carbohydrates, 11g fat, 45mg cholesterol, 260mg sodium
*not included in nutritional analysis

Estimated Prep Time: . . . . .10 minutes
Estimated Cooking Time: . . . . .16 minutes
Total: . . . . .26 minutes

Seafood

SHRIMP PAELLA

This dish will work great as a side dish, but can also be a main dish. Try adding some of your favorite shellfish for a great one-pot dinner.

Serves 2

Ingredients

1 pound medium-sized shrimp, cleaned and peeled (reserve shells)
1/4 cup tomato paste (or puree)
1-2 cloves garlic
Pinch of saffron
1 cup short-grain rice
1 3/4 cups hot "shrimp water"
1 cup green beans and/ or lima beans
2 tablespoons olive oil

Directions

In saucepan, lightly cook green beans (or lima beans) in salted water. In another pan, boil only the shells in salted water for 10 minutes to make the "shrimp water".

In pressure cooker, add 1/4 cup olive oil with tomato paste and stir until hot. Reduce heat; add rice, green beans, saffron and shrimp. Mix well and add "shrimp water".

Close lid, bring to high pressure, then lower heat and cook for 8 minutes. Remove from heat and let the pressure release naturally. Remove the lid and serve.

Approximate Nutritional Information Per Serving

600 calories, 43g protein, 69g carbohydrates, 16g fat, 325mg cholesterol, 390mg sodium

Estimated Prep Time: . . . .*5 minutes*
Estimated Cooking Time: . . . .*18 minutes*
Total: . . . .*23 minutes*

SEAFOOD GUMBO

Gumbo is a traditional American staple that originated in the South, but many varieties have sprung up nationwide. This recipe calls for a multitude of ingredients but by using the pressure cooker you can save up to 45 minutes versus traditional cooking.

Serves 10

Ingredients

1 1/4 cups flour
3/4 cup vegetable oil
1 cup diced white onions
1/2 cup diced celery
1 cup diced green bell pepper
4 cloves garlic, minced
2 tablespoons peanut oil
6 plum tomatoes, peeled, seeded and diced
3 bay leaves
1 teaspoon cayenne pepper
1/2 teaspoon onion powder
1/2 teaspoon garlic powder
1 teaspoon crushed dried thyme
1 teaspoon paprika
1 teaspoon celery seeds
1 pound andouille sausage or 1 pound hot Italian sausage
2 quarts chicken stock
2 dozen raw shrimp, shells off, tails on
2 dozen cooked crawfish tails, 6 crawfish reserved, for garnish
1/2 pound lump crab meat
2 dozen oysters, shucked
Salt and black pepper, to taste*

Directions

In a skillet over medium heat, combine flour with vegetable oil to make roux. Stir continuously for several minutes until dark brown color with nutty aroma is achieved. In the pressure cooker, sauté onions, celery, peppers and garlic in peanut oil until vegetables are soft approximately 10-15 minutes. Add tomatoes, spices, sausage and chicken stock.

Slowly add 2/3 to 1 cup of roux, 1 tablespoon at a time. When desired thickness is reached, add shrimp, crawfish, crabmeat and oysters. Close lid and bring to high pressure. Cook for 10 minutes. Release pressure using the cold water release method. Serve over rice or pasta.

Approximate Nutritional Information Per Serving

822 calories, 36g protein, 35g carbohydrates, 58g fat, 165mg cholesterol, 1074mg sodium
*not included in nutritional analysis

Estimated Prep Time: . . . .*10 minutes*
Estimated Cooking Time: . . . .*25 minutes*
Total: . . . .*35 minutes*

FRESH STEAMED LOBSTER

Pressure cookers easily replace the need to have a separate steamer. The lobster made in your cooker will be succulent and tender after only 3 minutes under high pressure.

Serves 1

Ingredients

4 cups water
1 1-1/2 pound lobster
Seaweed (optional)*

Directions

Put 4 cups of water in a 6 quart or larger pressure cooker. Add seaweed to the bottom of the cooker (if desired), then place 1 1-1/2 pound lobster on top of seaweed.

Close cooker and bring to high pressure, then lower heat and cook lobster for 3 minutes. When cooking time is up, release pressure using cold-water release method.

Open cooker, and enjoy!

Approximate Nutritional Information Per Serving

60 calories, 11g protein, 2g carbohydrates, 0g fat, 40mg cholesterol, 200mg sodium
*not included in nutritional analysis

Estimated Prep Time: . . . . .0 minutes
Estimated Cooking Time: . . . . .3 minutes
Total: . . . . .3 minutes

SALMON MARINATED IN RASPBERRY SAUCE WITH HERBS

Tangy raspberry vinaigrette offers an excellent balance to the delicately flavored salmon in this dish. Serve the fish over angel hair pasta or with plain couscous on the side.

Serves 6

Ingredients

6 salmon steaks (1 inch thick)
1 pint raspberry vinegar
   (see directions below)
2 tablespoons olive oil
4 leeks, cut into % inch slices
2 garlic cloves, crushed
2 tablespoons minced fresh parsley
1 cup bottled clam juice
2 tablespoons fresh lemon juice
1 teaspoon sherry
1 teaspoon salt
1/2 teaspoon white pepper
1/3 cup chopped fresh dill
Fresh raspberries, as garnish*

Directions

Marinate salmon steaks in raspberry vinegar, cover them and refrigerate them for at least 2 hours. Heat oil in pressure cooker. Add leeks, garlic and parsley and sauté for 2 minutes. Add clam juice, lemon juice, sherry, salt, pepper and dill; stir well. Remove salmon steaks from raspberry vinegar marinade and place in cooking liquid. Close lid, bring to high pressure, then lower heat and cook for 3 minutes. Release pressure using automatic or cold-water release method according to manufacturer's directions and remove lid.Transfer salmon steaks to serving platter. Arrange leeks around steaks and garnish with fresh raspberries.

Raspberry Vinegar:

In large stainless steel pan, place 2 pints ripe red raspberries. Cover them with one pint of cider vinegar. Let stand in cool place for 3 days. Strain liquid and store in sterile, well-corked glass bottle.
Note: Raspberry vinegar can also be found in select grocery stores.

Approximate Nutritional Information Per Serving

820 calories, 81g protein, 18g carbohydrates, 46g fat, 265mg cholesterol, 720mg sodium
*not included in nutritional analysis

Estimated Prep Time: . . . . .5 minutes
Estimated Cooking Time: . . . . .5 minutes
Total: . . . . .10 minutes

TUNA STEAKS IN OLIVE OIL

Marinating the tuna in this recipe is the key to the flavor of this dish. Be sure to marinate you tuna steaks for the full amount of time recommended to achieve maximum results.

Serves 8

Ingredients

2 pounds tuna steaks, 1" thick
2/3 cup extra virgin olive oil
2 cloves garlic, crushed
2 tablespoons coarsely chopped parsley
4 bay leaves
2 teaspoons salt
Pinch crushed red pepper flakes
1 cup water
2 teaspoons minced parsley
1 lemon, cut into wedges

Directions

One hour before steaming tuna, prepare marinade in a small bowl. Mix together olive oil, garlic, parsley, bay leaves, salt and red pepper. Set aside. Pour the water in the pressure cooker. Lightly grease the steaming basket with the vegetable oil. Place as many tuna steaks in the basket as can fit in a single layer. It will be necessary to steam in at least two batches.

Close lid and bring to high pressure. Cook for 3 minutes. Release pressure using the cold-water release method and carefully remove the steamer basket. Place the steaks on a platter and prick each steak a few times. Pour the marinade over the tuna through a strainer. Spoon marinated herbs over tuna steaks and marinate tuna for 2 hours.

Garnish tuna with minced parsley and lemon wedges. Serve over bed of steamed spinach or over a crisp spinach salad.

Approximate Nutritional Information Per Serving

280 calories, 19g protein, 1g carbohydrates, 19g fat, 53mg cholesterol, 625mg sodium
*not included in nutritional analysis

Estimated Prep Time: . . . . .5 minutes
Estimated Cooking Time: . . . . .6 minutes
Total: . . . . .11 minutes

SAVORY FISH CHOWDER

Rich and creamy, this special fish chowder is bursting with flavor and aroma. Serve with crusty bread on the side for dipping.

Serves 4

Ingredients

3 tablespoons olive oil
1 cup finely chopped onion
1 cup finely chopped celery
1 cup finely chopped carrot
1 1/2 cups peeled chopped tomato
1 teaspoon finely chopped garlic
1/2 cup flour
1/2 teaspoon cinnamon
1/2 teaspoon marjoram
1/2 teaspoon oregano
4 pints fish stock
1 cup half and half or light cream
2 cups cooked, flaked white fish meat
1-ounce black rum (Goslings, if available)
1-ounce Worcestershire sauce
1 1/2 tsp. hot sauce
Salt and pepper, to taste*

Directions

Heat the olive oil in the pressure cooker. Add all the chopped vegetables, tomato and garlic and sauté for 5 minutes. Stir frequently.

Add the flour, cinnamon and herbs and continue to cook for 2 minutes over medium low heat, stirring constantly to prevent roux from burning. Add the fish stock and cream and stir well. Crumble the fish into the pan with the rum, Worcestershire sauce and hot sauce.

Close the lid, bring to high pressure and cook for 20 minutes. Release pressure using the cold water release method. Stir well and add salt and pepper, if needed.

Approximate Nutritional Information Per Serving

520 calories, 31g protein, 40g carbohydrates, 25g fat, 50mg cholesterol, 200mg sodium
*not included in nutritional analysis

Estimated Prep Time: . . . . .10 minutes
Estimated Cooking Time: . . . . .27 minutes
Total: . . . . .37 minutes

GROUPER NEW ORLEANS

The grouper fish is very common in North America and is fairly easy to find at local seafood markets. Try serving this dish with rice or plain French bread on the side.

Serves 4

Ingredients

2 tablespoons oil
1 small onion, chopped
1 clove garlic, crushed
1 stalk celery, chopped
1 green pepper, chopped
1 16-ounce can tomatoes
1 tablespoon tomato paste
1 teaspoon sugar
pinch of basil
1/2 teaspoon chili powder
4 grouper fillets, in cubes

Directions

Heat oil in pressure cooker and sauté the onion, garlic, celery and green pepper for 2-3 minutes.

Stir in tomatoes, including the juice with water added to make up 1 1/4 cups. Add the tomato paste, sugar, basil, chili powder and grouper pieces.

Bring the cooker to high pressure, then lower heat and cook for 4 minutes. Release pressure using cold-water release method, open lid and serve.

Approximate Nutritional Information Per Serving

300 calories, 41g protein, 12g carbohydrates, 9g fat, 75mg cholesterol, 290mg sodium

Estimated Prep Time: . . . . .10 minutes
Estimated Cooking Time: . . . . .7 minutes
Total: .17 minutes

SEAFOOD MEDLEY

This dish is perfect for impressing a crowd. Serving in the loaf of bread is not only unique but also adds to the flavor of the recipe.

Serves 6

Ingredients

2 (1 1/2 pound) whole lobsters
1 pound live Littleneck or Manila clams
1 lemon
1/4 cup white wine
1/4 cup water
1 pound sea scallops
1/2-cup cognac
1 shallot, finely shopped
2 cups chilled butter, diced
Salt and pepper, to taste
1 large round loaf semolina bread
Parsley, finely chopped, for garnish

Directions

Place clams in a bowl of water with juice of one lemon. Let sit for 1 hour to remove any dirt or sediment from inside clams. Put lobster and clams in the steamer basket on top of trivet inside in the pressure cooker. Add 1/4 cup water. Close lid, bring to high pressure and cook for 7 minutes. Release pressure using the cold water release method. Remove the lobster and clams. Reserve the juices. Crack and separate the claws and tails from the lobster discard the shells. In a shallow sauté pan, add the wine, water, and scallops. Cook on medium heat until the scallops are done. Reserve the juices. Combine the reserved seafood juices which should equal 1 1/2 cups liquid. If there is too little liquid, supplement with water. In the pressure cooker, add the reserved juices, cognac, and shallots, and reduce by half. Remove from heat add 2 pieces of butter. Whisk until melted and return to medium heat continue to whisk while adding the butter, the sauce should thicken to the pouring consistency of cream. Add the salt and pepper, to taste. Cut the top off the loaf of bread and hollow it out. Leave an inch thick crust on the sides and bottom. Fill the bread hollow with the seafood and top with the cognac sauce. Garnish with a sprinkle of parsley. Serve immediately once assembled.

Approximate Nutritional Information Per Serving

1030 calories, 53g protein, 43g carbohydrates, 66g fat, 295mg cholesterol, 1660mg sodium
*not included in nutritional analysis

Estimated Prep Time: . . . . .1 hour
Estimated Cooking Time: . . . . .7 minutes
Total: .1 h 7 minutes

STEAMED MUSSELS

Less is more when it comes to cooking mussels! Use only fresh mussels, which are tightly closed when you buy them. If you can't find fresh mussels, make something else! Serve with slices of freshly grilled garlic to soak up the delicious broth.

Serves 8

Ingredients

4 pounds mussels
2 tablespoons olive oil
1 shallot, minced
2 garlic cloves, shaved
4 sprigs fresh thyme
1/2 cup dry white wine
1 lemon, juiced
1 cup chicken broth, low-sodium
Pinch red pepper flakes
1 tomato, peeled, seeded and cut in large dice
1/2 cup roughly chopped parsley
2 tablespoons unsalted butter

Directions

Rinse the mussels under cold running water while scrubbing with a vegetable brush. Discard any with broken shells.

Heat oil in the pressure cooker. Sauté the shallot, garlic and thyme. Add the mussels and toss well. Add wine, lemon juice, chicken broth and red pepper flakes. Close lid, bring to high pressure and cook for 4 minutes. Release pressure using the automatic release method.

Toss in the tomato, parsley and butter, and simmer uncovered for another three minutes to soften. The tomatoes should keep their shape. Serve with grilled garlic bread.

Approximate Nutritional Information Per Serving

270 calories, 28g protein, 11g carbohydrates, 12g fat, 73mg cholesterol, 670mg sodium

Estimated Prep Time: . . . . .5 minutes
Estimated Cooking Time: . . . . .7 minutes
Total: .12 minutes

CLAM CHOWDER

A hearty blend of vegetables and clams blend with a little added spice in this chowder. This soup tastes even better the next day.

Serves 6

Ingredients

10 ounces fresh clam meat
4 tablespoons (1/2 stick) unsalted butter
1 1/2 medium onions, diced
4 cups clam juice
2 cups heavy cream
1 large carrot, peeled and diced
1 stalk of celery, diced
1 large red or white potato, peeled and diced
1/4 teaspoon freshly ground black
2 dashes of Tabasco
Juice of 1/2 lemon

Beurre Manie:

1 tablespoon softened, unsalted butter
1 tablespoon all-purpose flour

Directions

Roughly chop clam meat and reserve. Melt butter in pressure cooker over low heat. Cook onions until soft, about 5 minutes. Add clams and cook an additional 3 minutes, stirring occasionally to avoid browning.

Add clam juice, cream, carrots, celery, and potato. Close pressure cooker lid and bring to high pressure. Cook for 7 minutes. Release pressure using the cold water release method and open cooker.

Make Beurre Manie by mixing butter and flour together with your fingers to form a smooth paste. Press onto ends of a whisk and stir into soup until completely and evenly dispersed. Stir in remaining ingredients, taste and adjust seasonings, and serve immediately.

Approximate Nutritional Information Per Serving

490 calories, 19g protein, 15g carbohydrates, 40g fat, 165mg cholesterol, 340mg sodium

Estimated Prep Time: . . . . .10 minutes
Estimated Cooking Time: . . . . .15 minutes
Total: . . . . .25 minutes

Vegetables

STUFFED TOMATOES

You can substitute the ground lamb in this dish with any ground meat. To cut the fat, try using ground turkey meat.

Serves 6

Ingredients
- 6 ripe tomatoes
- 2 cups low-sodium beef broth
- 2 teaspoons garlic
- 1 teaspoon salt
- 2 teaspoons parsley
- 1 teaspoon dill
- 1 large onion, minced
- 1/3 cup chopped parsley
- 1 pound ground lamb
- 1 cup white rice (long-grain)
- 1 cup breadcrumbs

Directions

Cut and remove the top of each tomato; scoop out pulp and juice, leaving tomato shells. Mash pulp and add garlic, salt, parsley and dill. Set aside.

In the pressure cooker, sauté onions in oil for 1 1/2 minutes. Crumble ground meat and add it to the pressure cooker with the rice and tomato mixture. Stir.

Close lid, bring to high pressure, then lower and cook for 8 minutes. Release pressure using the cold-water release method and open lid.

Spoon mixture into tomato shells that have been placed in a baking pan. Top with breadcrumbs, and drizzle butter over top. Place tomato shells in a preheated broiler and bake until tops are browned, approximately 1 1/2 minutes.

Approximate Nutritional Information Per Serving
380 calories, 20g protein, 47g carbohydrates, 12g fat, 50mg cholesterol, 630mg sodium

Estimated Prep Time: . . . . .10 minutes
Estimated Cooking Time: . . . . .12 minutes
Total: . . . . .22 minutes

VEGETABLE FIESTA

A simple blend of ordinary vegetables is transformed into something spectacular in this recipe. If all vegetables are not available to you, try substituting with what is in season for your own variation.

Serves 4

Ingredients
- 1 cup low sodium chicken stock
- 1 cup tomato sauce
- 1 cup long grain rice
- 1 teaspoon olive oil
- 2 medium sized zucchini or squash, cut into 1/4" round slices
- 1/2 pound Great Northern beans, or to preference
- 1 small head cabbage {white is preferred), cut into 1 " pieces
- 1/8 teaspoon salt
- 1 cup corn {optional)*

Directions

Add chicken stock, olive oil, tomato sauce, and rice to pressure cooker, close lid and bring to high pressure, then lower heat and cook for 5 minutes.

Release pressure using cold-water release method, open lid and add zucchini or squash, beans, cabbage and salt. Close lid, bring to high pressure, then lower heat and cook for 20 minutes, until cabbage is tender.

Release pressure using cold-water release method, open lid and add corn, if desired. Serve.

Approximate Nutritional Information Per Serving
500 calories, 22g protein, 100g carbohydrates, 3.5g fat, 0mg cholesterol, 530mg sodium
*not included in nutritional analysis

Estimated Prep Time: . . . . .5 minutes
Estimated Cooking Time: . . . . .25 minutes
Total: .30 minutes

COUNTRY STYLE POTATOES

For simple and tasty potatoes, try this recipe as an easy side dish.

Serves 4

Ingredients

1 tablespoon olive oil
1/4 pound fresh mushrooms, stems trimmed, sliced
1/2 cup finely chopped onion
1/2 teaspoon salt
1/8 teaspoon pepper
1/2 cup chicken stock or water
4 cups potatoes in 1/2 inch slices
2 tablespoons minced parsley

Directions

Heat the oil in the pressure cooker over medium high heat and sauté the mushrooms and onions until the onions are wilted. Mix in all the remaining ingredients.

Close the lid and bring to high pressure, then lower heat and cook for 5 minutes.

Release pressure with the cold water release method and remove the lid. Serve.

Approximate Nutritional Information Per Serving

170 calories, 4g protein, 30g carbohydrates, 4g fat, 0mg cholesterol, 430mg sodium

Estimated Prep Time: . . . . .5 minutes
Estimated Cooking Time: . . . . .10 minutes
Total: . . . . .15 minutes

STUFFED ARTICHOKES

Versatile and delicious, artichokes are packed with vitamins and nutrients. Unfortunately, many people rarely cook with them because of the time it takes. Using your pressure cooker will help you dramatically decrease the time you will spend steaming these healthy delights.

Serves 4

Ingredients

4 large artichokes (clip each leaf and cut off stems)
2 slices of white bread per artichoke (stale bread is the best)
1/2 Cup Italian breadcrumbs
2 tablespoons olive oil
Salt, black pepper and garlic to taste*
3 tablespoons Parmesan cheese

Directions

Remove stems from artichokes and peel and chop them into small pieces. Put in large bowl.

Cut bread in small pieces and add to stems. Take remaining ingredients and mix together, adding enough water to mixture to hold ingredients together. The more spices added, the tastier the recipe.

Wash artichokes, spread center open and put stuffing inside. Put artichokes in pressure cooker with enough water to cover 1/3 of artichokes.

Close lid, bring to high pressure, then lower heat and cook for 12 minutes. Release pressure using the automatic release method, open lid and serve while hot.

Approximate Nutritional Information Per Serving

390 calories, 15g protein, 60g carbohydrates, 12g fat, 5mg, cholesterol, 780mg sodium
*not included in nutritional analysis

Estimated Prep Time: . . . . .10 minutes
Estimated Cooking Time: . . . . .12 minutes
Total: . . . . .22 minutes

TRADITIONAL VEGETABLE STEW

Hearty and filling, this vegetable stew is perfect for a chilly evening. You can easily substitute the vegetable below for whatever is in season.

Serves 4

Ingredients

1 1/2 cups vegetable stock
1 tablespoon low-sodium soy sauce
1 onion, chopped
1 red bell pepper, diced
4 large garlic cloves, minced
1 pound (about 4 cups) butternut squash or 20 oz. package fresh cut butternut squash
1 15-ounce can chopped tomatoes
1/2 teaspoon oregano
1 1/2 teaspoons chili powder
1/2 teaspoon cumin
1/4 teaspoon black pepper
1 15-ounce can kidney beans
1 1/2 cups fresh or frozen corn

Directions

Heat 1/2 cup vegetable stock and soy sauce in pressure cooker pot, then add onion, bell pepper and garlic and cook over medium heat until the onion is translucent and most of the vegetable stock has evaporated. Cut the squash in half and remove seeds, then peel and cut into 1/2-inch cubes.

Add squash cubes to onion mixture, along with chopped tomatoes, remaining 1 cup water, oregano, chili powder, cumin and pepper. Close lid, bring up to high pressure, then lower heat and cook for 4 minutes. Release pressure using cold-water release method. Add kidney beans in their liquid and the corn. Cook without lid on for 5 minutes longer over medium heat. Serve warm with your favorite bread.

Approximate Nutritional Information Per Serving

270 calories, 14g protein, 58g carbohydrates, 2g fat, 0mg cholesterol, 670mg sodium

Estimated Prep Time: . . . .*5 minutes*
Estimated Cooking Time: . . . .*9 minutes*
Total: . . . .*14 minutes*

HERBED GARLIC MASHED POTATOES

These potatoes are excellent as an accompaniment to any meal. The rosemary and thyme combine for an unusual, yet tasty mingling of flavors.

6 servings

Ingredients

3 large potatoes, peeled and cubed
1 cup chicken broth with garlic seasoning
1 cup warm skim milk
2 tablespoons olive oil
1 tablespoon minced thyme
1/2 teaspoon garlic powder
1/2 teaspoon dried rosemary, crushed
1/2 teaspoon salt
1/2 teaspoon pepper

Directions

Add potatoes and broth to the pressure cooker. Close lid, bring to high pressure, then lower heat and cook for 6 minutes.

Release pressure with the cold water release method. Open lid and drain broth, leaving only 1/4 cup of broth remaining.

Add the warm milk and olive oil. Beat with mixer until potatoes are fluffy. Add the herbs, salt and pepper. Serve while hot.

Approximate Nutritional Information Per Serving

160 calories, 4g protein, 26g carbohydrates, 5g fat, 0mg cholesterol, 390mg sodium

Estimated Prep Time: . . . .*5 minutes*
Estimated Cooking Time: . . . .*6 minutes*
Total: . . . .*11 minutes*

SPAGHETTI SQUASH

Serves 6

Ingredients
2 Spaghetti squash, halved
1 pound Italian Sausage, removed from casing
1 cup spaghetti sauce
1 cup mild, thick chunky salsa
2 tablespoon horseradish sauce
2 cups very ripe chopped tomatoes
1 tablespoon minced garlic in olive oil
Shredded cheddar cheese

Directions
Place squash in pressure cooker, cut side down in water to cover. Close lid, bring to high pressure, then lower heat and cook for 14 minutes until tender.

While squash is cooking, sauté sausage in skillet for 15 minutes under low heat. Do not overbrown. Once sausage is cooked, add spaghetti sauce, salsa and horseradish, stirring well. Cook on low heat for 5 minutes, then add tomatoes and garlic, bringing to a boil. Set aside and keep hot.

Release pressure from cooker, drain and remove squash from shell with a fork. Place on an ovenproof platter, then top with sauce and cheddar cheese. Heat in the 325° F. oven until cheese is melted.

Approximate Nutritional Information Per Serving
310 calories, 15g protein, 20g carbohydrates, 20g fat, 50mg cholesterol, 1050mg sodium

GREEN BEANS AND POTATOES

Serves 2

Ingredients
2 boxes frozen green beans (10 oz. ea.)
1/4 medium onion, diced
4 medium-sized potatoes
1/2 cup water
Freshly ground black pepper
1 tablespoon butter

Directions
Peel potatoes, cut into quarters, then place in pressure cooker with onions, frozen green beans and water. Close lid, bring up to high pressure, then lower heat and cook for 3-5 minutes. Release pressure using cold-water release method.

Place potatoes and green beans in a bowl or platter and season with freshly ground black pepper. Add a tablespoon of butter to dish.

Approximate Nutritional Information Per Serving
170 calories, 5g protein, 33g carbohydrates, 3.5g fat, 10mg cholesterol, 40mg sodium

GERMAN POTATO SALAD

Tangy and spicy, the vinegar and mustard in this potato salad add an exceptional flavor to the potatoes. You can also try making this salad using new red potatoes with the skins on for a colorful alternative.

Serves 8

Ingredients

- 3 pounds large boiling potatoes (about 6)
- 3/4 cup water
- 1/2 pound of lean bacon (about 8 slices), cut crosswise into 1/2-inch pieces
- 1 cup finely chopped onion
- 1 cup thinly sliced celery
- 1 tablespoon sugar
- 2 tablespoons all-purpose flour
- 1 teaspoon celery seeds
- 1 tablespoon Dijon-style mustard
- 6 tablespoons cider vinegar
- 1/2 cup water
- 3 hard-boiled large eggs, chopped
- 1/3 cup chopped dill pickles
- 1/2 cup thinly sliced scallion greens
- Salt and pepper to taste

Directions

Quarter the potatoes lengthwise and cut them crosswise into 1/2 inch pieces. In steamer basket, add potatoes and place in pressure cooker with water. Close lid; bring to high pressure, then lower heat and pressure cook for 5 minutes. Release pressure with the cold water release method, open lid, drain water and remove potatoes to bowl. Put eggs steamer basket or egg poaching tray, put in cooker and add cold water to cover eggs. Bring to a rolling boil (do not add pressure cooker lid). Reduce to simmer and let them cook for 10-12 minutes. Plunge into cold water at once. Once cooked, chop into pieces. In a large heavy skillet, cook bacon over moderate heat, stirring, until it is crisp, then transfer to paper towels to drain. Pour off all but 4 tablespoons of the fat, and add to skillet onion and celery -cook the mixture over moderately low heat, stirring, until onion is softened. Add the sugar, flour and celery seeds, and cook for 30 seconds, stirring often. Stir in the mustard, vinegar, and 1/2 cup of water, bring mixture to a boil, stirring, then lower heat and simmer for 2 minutes, or until mixture is thickened. Season the dressing with salt and pepper, pour it over the potatoes, and stir in the eggs, pickles, bacon and scallion greens. Serve the salad warm.

Approximate Nutritional Information Per Serving

250 calories, 12g protein, 42g carbohydrates, 4.5g fat, 95mg cholesterol, 610mg sodium

Estimated Prep Time: . . . . .10 minutes
Estimated Cooking Time: . . . . .18 minutes
Total: .28 minutes

APPLE POTATO SALAD

Healthy and nutritious, the salad is great for a day at the park because it holds well even if it is not refrigerated. Make it the day before for a more mature flavor.

Serves 4

Ingredients

- 4 small new potatoes
- 1 Delicious Apple
- 4 celery stalks, finely chopped
- 1/2 cup no-oil Creamy Dill dressing
- 1/4 teaspoon dill

Directions

Slice the potatoes into bite-sized pieces. Place in pressure cooker with 1/2 cup water. Close lid, bring to high pressure, and cook for 4 minutes. Release pressure using cold-water release method. Drain and place in a pan of ice water.

Peel the apple and slice into bite-sized pieces (sprinkle with lemon juice so it won't brown).

Combine all ingredients and mix with dressing and dill. Chill several hours.

Approximate Nutritional Information Per Serving

140 calories, 3g protein, 33g carbohydrates, 0g fat, 0mg cholesterol, 180mg sodium

Estimated Prep Time: . . . . .5 minutes
Estimated Cooking Time: . . . . .4 minutes
Total: .9 minutes

Beans & Grains

STEAMED RICE

Your basic rice recipe is now even easier and faster than traditional cooking. The butter can easily be omitted for a low-fat version.

4 Servings

Ingredients
3 tablespoons olive oil 1 cup long-grain rice
2 cups low sodium chicken broth or water
1 tablespoon butter
salt and pepper, to taste*

Directions
Heat oil in pressure cooker. Stir in rice, and then add broth or water.

Close lid, bring up to high pressure, then lower heat and cook 8 minutes. Release pressure, open lid, add butter, plus salt and pepper to taste. Mix thoroughly. Serve at once while hot.

Approximate Nutritional Information Per Serving
250 calories, 5g protein, 41g carbohydrates, 8g fat, 10mg cholesterol, 85mg sodium
*not included in nutritional analysis

Estimated Prep Time: . . . .*0 minutes*
Estimated Cooking Time: . . . .*8 minutes*
Total: . . . .*8 minutes*

SUNDRIED TOMATO RISOTTO

Sundried tomatoes work well with the flavor of the garlic and Parmesan cheese in this unconventional risotto recipe. Serve this side dish as an accompaniment to grilled whitefish or chicken.

Serves 6

Ingredients
1 ounce sundried tomatoes
1 cup water
2 1/2 cups chicken broth
1 cup finely chopped onion
1 garlic clove, minced
4 tablespoons olive oil
1 cup Arborio rice
1/4 cup freshly grated Parmesan
finely chopped fresh parsley leaves for sprinkling risotto if desired

Directions
In the pressure cooker, simmer the tomatoes in the water for 1 minute, drain them, reserving the liquid, and chop them.

Cook the onion and the garlic in the oil over moderately low heat, stirring, until they are softened, add the rice, stirring until each grain is coated with oil, and stir in the tomatoes. Combine the reserved cooking liquid and the broth; add the liquid to the cooker and bring to a simmer.

Close the lid, bring to high pressure and cook for 6 minutes. Release the pressure with the cold water release method. Open the cooker and taste the risotto. It should be barely tender (al dente). If necessary, return to medium heat add a small amount of liquid and stir until rice is slightly tender.

Stir in the Parmesan and salt and pepper to taste and sprinkle the risotto with the parsley. Let stand 1 minute before serving.

Approximate Nutritional Information Per Serving
220 calories, 6g protein, 25g carbohydrates, 11g fat, 5mg cholesterol, 380mg sodium

Estimated Prep Time: . . . .*5 minutes*
Estimated Cooking Time: . . . .*10 minutes*
Total: . . . .*15 minutes*

BBQ BEANS

Beans are a staple in many households. The drawback to using dried beans as opposed to the canned variety has simply been time constraints. With your pressure cooker you can have your own home cooked beans in 70% less time. This recipe calls for use of the quick-soak method. Using this method cuts even more time off cooking.

Serves 4-6

Ingredients

1 pound dry navy or small white beans, rinsed and quick soaked
1 cups chopped white onions
1 cups chopped red onions
1/8 cup minced garlic
1/4 cup red wine vinegar
1 tablespoons Dijon mustard
1/4 cup soy sauce
1cups dark brown sugar
1/4 cup Worcestershire sauce
1/4 cup ketchup
1 tablespoons dark chili powder
1 chipotle chile, chopped
1/2 pound canned plum tomatoes, drained and chopped
1/4 cup molasses
3 cups water or chicken stock
1 tablespoon olive oil
1 T. honey
Salt and pepper, to taste

Directions

To quick soak the beans:
Place the rinsed beans in the steamer basket on top of steamer trivet and put inside the pressure cooker. Add 6 cups of water. Close lid, bring to high pressure and cook for 2 minutes. Release pressure using the cold water release method. Remove beans and rinse again. Your beans are now ready to be cooked.

Return the beans to the cooker and add the olive oil and water or stock. Close the lid, bring to high pressure and cook for 8 minutes. Release pressure using the automatic release method.

Drain the beans and return them to the cooker. Beans may still remain a little hard. Combine the remaining ingredients. Close the lid again, bring to high pressure and cook for 15 minutes. Release pressure using the cold water release method.

Estimated Prep Time: . . . . .5 minutes
Estimated Cooking Time: . . . . .25 minutes
Total: . . . . .30 minutes

MEDITERRANEAN RISOTTO

Twelve minutes is all it takes to prepare this savory and tasty risotto dish!

Serves 4

Ingredients

1 6 1/2 oz. jar artichoke hearts (quartered), drained, reserve liquid/oil
2-3 cloves garlic, peeled and minced
1 cup Arborio rice
2 1/4 cups rich vegetable stock 8 large stuffed olives
2 roasted red peppers (from jar), drained and patted dry
1/4 cup sliced sun dried tomatoes (either packed in oil/drained or reconstituted in water/drained)
1/4 pound Gruyere cheese diced
3 tablespoons Italian parsley, chopped
Pepper

Directions

Heat 2 tablespoons of artichoke liquid/oil in pressure cooker over medium-high heat. Add garlic and sauté for 30 seconds. Add the rice and sauté, stirring often, until lightly golden. Pour in stock. Stir well.

Position the lid and lock in place. Bring to high pressure then lower heat and cook for 7 minutes.

While risotto is cooking, slice the olives and roasted red peppers.

Remove risotto from heat and release pressure using automatic or cold-water release method. Stir in artichoke hearts, olives, roasted red peppers, sun-dried tomatoes, Gruyere cheese, and 1 tablespoon of reserved liquid.

Let risotto sit in cooker until cheese has melted. Stir one more time and sprinkle with Italian parsley and pepper. Serve at once.

Approximate Nutritional Information Per Serving

330 calories, 13g protein, 37g carbohydrates, 14g fat, 30 mg cholesterol, 790mg sodium

Estimated Prep Time: . . . . .5 minutes
Estimated Cooking Time: . . . . .7 minutes
Total: . . . . .12 minutes

RISOTTO RAPIDO WITH RIOJA, SAFFRON AND PARSLEY

Complex flavors of Manchego cheese and Rioja wine blend perfectly with the other ingredients in this recipe. Colorful and fun, you will think you're at gourmet restaurant when you taste this wonderful risotto.

Serves 6

Ingredients

1 teaspoon saffron threads
1 tablespoon extra-virgin olive oil, plus additional for garnish
5 ounces shallots, trimmed and minced
3 cloves garlic, minced
2 1/2 cups Arborio rice
4 tablespoons fresh mint, torn, plus 1/2 cup for garnish
2 - 2 1/2 cups low-sodium vegetable broth
3 1/4 cups Rioja wine.
3/4 cup pitted imported green olives (optional), sliced, divided

Garnish:
3 ounces Manchego cheese, grated coarsely (or substitute with Pecorino cheese),
Fresh mint leaves and parsley oil
   (see below)

Directions

Infuse saffron by placing in 1/4 cup of warm stock and set aside. Heat one tablespoon of oil in a 6 quart or larger pressure cooker, then add shallots and garlic. Sauté until translucent, about 2 minutes. Add rice, 4 tablespoons mint, stirring to coat rice. Add the wine, 2 cups of broth, saffron, wine and half the olives. Close lid, bring up to high pressure and cook for 7 minutes. Release pressure using the cold-water release method. Stir thoroughly. If necessary, add salt and pepper to taste. The risotto should be very creamy. If not, add 1/2 cup more stock and cook one additional minute without pressure. Ladle portions of risotto into warmed shallow plates. Drizzle each portion with one teaspoon of parsley oil (see below). Garnish with cheese and mint leaves. Serve immediately while hot.

Parsley Oil:
1/4 cup extra-virgin Spanish olive oil, warmed
3 tablespoons chopped parsley, coarsely chopped

Directions

Warm 1/4 cup olive oil in a small saucepan until hot but not scalding. Transfer to a mini processor or blender and blend with the parsley and mint leaves. Strain through a fine strainer into a small jar. You will only need 6 teaspoons for this recipe. Refrigerate remainder for another use.

Approximate Nutritional Information Per Serving

440 calories, 10g protein, 58g carbohydrates, 10g fat, 15mg cholesterol, 970mg sodium

Estimated Prep Time: . . . . .10 minutes
Estimated Cooking Time: . . . . .10 minutes
Total: . . . . .20 minutes

BEAN AND PEPPER SALAD

Feeling hot today? The blend of spicy chilies and peppers in this dish is sure to excite your taste buds and get your blood flowing.

Serves 4

Ingredients

- 3/4 cup dried black beans
- 3/4 cup dried red or kidney beans
- 1 yellow bell pepper
- 1 red bell pepper
- 1 fresh poblano chili pepper
- 1/4 cup red wine vinegar
- 1 teaspoon salt
- 1/2 teaspoon freshly ground black pepper
- 1 canned chipotle chili pepper in vinegar or in adobo sauce, stemmed, seeded, and minced (optional)
- 2/3 cup olive oil
- 1 red (Spanish) onion, finely diced

Directions

Sort through beans and discard any stones or other foreign matter. Rinse well. Place beans in pressure cooker, turn on heat to medium-high, bring to high pressure, then lower heat and cook for 18 minutes. Release pressure using natural release method.

Open lid and drain beans in a colander and spread them on plate to cool slightly. Remove the stems, seeds and ribs from the bell peppers and poblano chili. Cut the peppers into 1/4-inch dice, or a size as small as the cooked beans.

In a large bowl, whisk together the vinegar, salt, black pepper and chipotle chili, if using. Slowly add the olive oil, whisking constantly. Toss in the diced peppers, onion and warm beans and mix well. Cover and refrigerate for at least two hours or as long as overnight. Serve the salad chilled.

Approximate Nutritional Information Per Serving

580 calories, 16g protein, 47g carbohydrates, 37g fat, 0mg cholesterol, 590mg sodium

```
Estimated Prep Time: . . . . . . . . . . .5 minutes
Estimated Cooking Time:  . . . . . . . .20 minutes
Total:  . . . . . . . . . . . . . . . . . . . .25 minutes
```

WHITE BEAN ESCAROLE SOUP

This soup is garlicky and packed with fiber and iron. Try serving is small bowls, topped with shredded cheese.

Serves 6

Ingredients

- 3 tablespoons olive oil
- 1 onion, finely chopped
- 2 carrots, finely chopped
- 3 cloves garlic, minced
- 6 cups chicken broth
- 1 pound white cannellini beans, quick soaked*
- 4 fresh sage leaves, finely sliced
- 8 ounces escarole or romaine lettuce, sliced thinly
- 1/4 cup chopped Italian parsley
- salt and pepper

Directions

Add the quick-soaked beans to the cooker and add one tablespoon of olive oil and 2 cups water or stock. Close the lid, bring to high pressure and cook for 8 minutes. Release pressure using the automatic release method. Remove and set aside. Heat olive oil in the pressure cooker. Add onion and carrots, cover and simmer 5 minutes or until tender. Add the garlic and sauté for a minute. Add _ the beans and mash with a potato masher. Add the other half of beans along with the broth and escarole. Close the lid, bring to high pressure and cook for 10 minutes. Release pressure using the automatic release method. Open lid, add parsley and sage and adjust seasoning. Simmer 5 minutes. Serve with bread and salad for a complete meal.

*To quick soak the beans:

Place the rinsed beans in the steamer basket on top of steamer trivet and put inside the pressure cooker. Add 6 cups of water. Close lid, bring to high pressure and cook for 2 minutes. Release pressure using the cold water release method. Remove beans and rinse again. Your beans are now ready to be cooked.

Approximate Nutritional Information Per Serving

360 calories, 22g protein, 52g carbohydrates, 8g fat, 0mg cholesterol, 510mg sodium

```
Estimated Prep Time: . . . . . . . . . . .5 minutes
Estimated Cooking Time:  . . . . . . . .28 minutes
Total:  . . . . . . . . . . . . . . . . . . . .33 minutes
```

BLACK BEANS AND CHORIZO SAUSAGE

Latin households are very familiar with this flavorful side dish. Chorizo is a spicy Spanish sausage, look for it in grocery stores and Latin markets.

Serves 8

Ingredients
1/2 tablespoon vegetable oil
1/4 pound dried Spanish chorizo sausage, finely chopped
1 cups chopped onions
1 small chili pepper, finely minced
salt
freshly ground black pepper
2 tablespoons chopped garlic
1/2 pound dried black beans
4 cups chicken stock
1 tablespoon butter

Directions
Add the oil to the pressure cooker. When the oil is hot add the sausage and brown for 2 minutes. Add the onions and peppers. Season with salt and pepper to taste and sauté for 3 to 4 minutes or until the vegetables are wilted.

Stir in the garlic and black beans. Sauté for 1 minute. Add the stock, close the lid, and bring to high pressure. Cook for 45 minutes. Release pressure using the cold water release method.

Open cooker, stir in the butter and re-season with salt and pepper.

Approximate Nutritional Information Per Serving
200 calories, 12g protein, 20g carbohydrates, 9g fat, 20g cholesterol, 250mg sodium

Estimated Prep Time: . . . . .5 minutes
Estimated Cooking Time: . . . . .45 minutes
Total: . . . . .50 minutes

RED BEANS AND RICE

This is an easy and delicious take on a Louisiana classic that you can prepare and cook in one hour! Try adding turkey kielbasa to add extra flavor.

Serves 8

Ingredients
1 pound dried red beans (quick soaked)
1 large yellow onion, diced
1 cup diced celery
1 cup chopped green pepper
4 garlic cloves, finely chopped or minced
4 bay leaves
4 T. parsley, chopped
2 tsp. Dried thyme, crushed
1 1/2 teaspoons salt
1/2 teaspoon crushed red pepper
1 teaspoon freshly ground black pepper
3/4 cup olive oil
3 to 4 cups water
2 to 3 cups cooked rice

Directions
Drain the beans, discarding the water, and set them aside in the pressure cooker.

Place the onion, celery, green pepper, garlic, bay leaves, and seasonings in a medium mixing bowl. Drizzle the olive oil over them and let the mixture sit at room temperature for at least 30 minutes.

Pour the olive oil and vegetables over the beans and let sit at room temperature for 10 to 15 minutes. Add enough of the water to cover the beans. Close the lid, bring to high pressure and cook for 40 minutes.

Remove the bay leaves and serve the hot beans over the rice.

Approximate Nutritional Information Per Serving
200 calories, 12g protein, 20g carbohydrates, 9g fat, 20g cholesterol, 250mg sodium

Estimated Prep Time: . . . . .5 minutes
Estimated Cooking Time: . . . . .55 minutes
Total: . . . . .1 hour

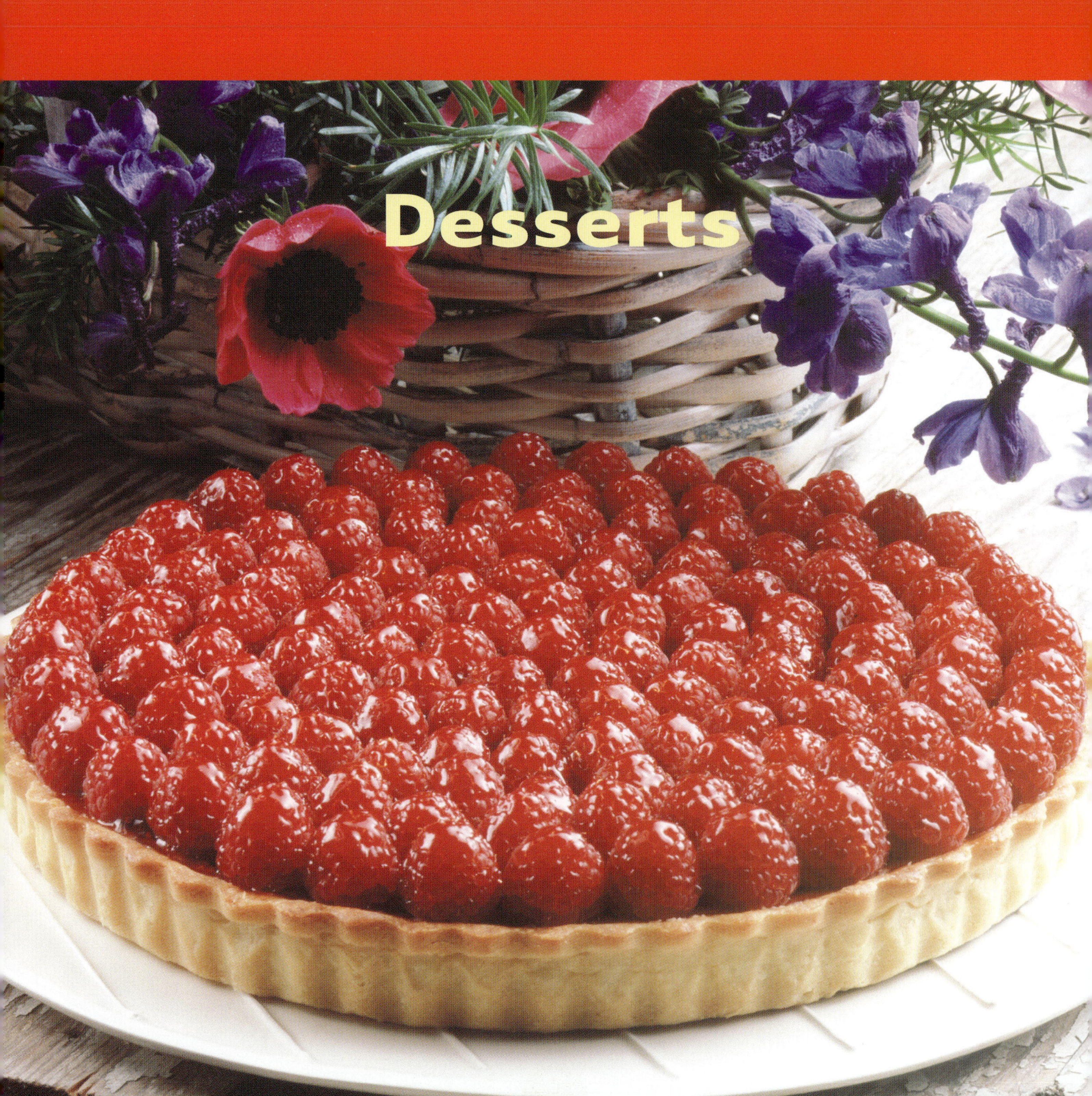

Desserts

CREAMY RICE PUDDING

This pudding comes out rich and velvety in the pressure cooker. If you like extra creamy rice pudding, try using short or medium grain rice.

Serves 6

Ingredients

- 1 cup long-grain rice
- 2 cups water
- 1/8 teaspoon nutmeg
- 1/3 cup honey
- 1/2 cup sugar
- 3/4 cup evaporated milk, preferably low-fat
- 1/2 cup milk (1% or skim milk reduces fat in recipe)
- 3 egg yolks
- 1/3 cup raisins
- 3/4 teaspoon vanilla extract
- Cinnamon or Nutmeg

Directions

In cooker, combine rice and water. Close lid, bring to high pressure, then lower heat and cook for 8 minutes.

Release pressure with the automatic release method and, open lid and add honey and sugar to rice mixture. Stir in evaporated milk, milk and egg yolks. Cook over medium heat for 3 minutes or until mixture thickens. Stir constantly.

Add raisins and vanilla extract. Spoon into serving glasses and sprinkle with cinnamon or nutmeg.

Approximate Nutritional Information Per Serving

330 calories, 7g protein, 70g carbohydrates, 3.5g fat, 110mg cholesterol, 45mg sodium

Estimated Prep Time: . . . . .5 minutes
Estimated Cooking Time: . . . . .11 minutes
Total: . . . . .16 minutes

SPICED APPLES

This is an excellent, yet simple dessert to serve following a heavy meat dish such as pork chops or pot roast.

Serves 4

Ingredients

- 5 apples, peeled, cored and cut into 1/2" slices
- 1 cup orange juice
- 3/4 Cup granulated sugar
- 1 cup firmly-packed brown sugar
- 1/4 teaspoon nutmeg
- 1 1/2 teaspoons cinnamon
- 1/2 teaspoon rum flavoring (optional)
- 2 tablespoons cornstarch
- 1/2 cup water

Directions

Combine apples, juice, sugar, brown sugar, nutmeg, cinnamon and rum flavoring in the pressure cooker.

Close lid, bring to high pressure, then lower heat and cook for 3 minutes. Release pressure using the cold-water release method. Remove lid.

Stir apples. Mix cornstarch with water and stir into apples. Cook over medium-high heat, stirring often, for 1 minute, or until juices become clear and shiny.

Serve over pound cake is desired.

Approximate Nutritional Information Per Serving

490 calories, 1g protein, 126g carbohydrates, 0.5g fat, 0mg cholesterol, 25mg sodium

Estimated Prep Time: . . . . .5 minutes
Estimated Cooking Time: . . . . .4 minutes
Total: . . . . .9 minutes

HEAVENLY CREAMY ALMOND FLAN

Almond and vanilla flavor this wonderful Spanish custard dish. This dessert is great to make ahead for special occasions.

Serves 4

Ingredients

1/2 cup sugar
1 cup milk
1/8 teaspoon salt
1 can (14 oz.) sweetened condensed milk
4 eggs
1 teaspoon vanilla
1/2 teaspoon almond extract
1/2 cup sliced almonds, as garnish

Directions

Over medium heat, place sugar in small heavy skillet and heat until sugar begins to melt and syrup turns golden. Immediately pour into a one-quart baking dish that fits into pressure cooker. Tilt dish in all directions to coat bottom and as much of the sides before syrup stops running; set aside.

In bowl or blender, mix remaining ingredients until smooth. Pour into prepared baking dish and cover tightly. Set covered dish into cooker; pour hot water into cooker to come half way up the sides of the baking dish.

Close lid; bring to high pressure, then lower heat and pressure cook for 10 minutes. Remove from stove and allow pressure to drop naturally.

Take flan out of the cooker, sprinkle with sliced almonds and serve warm or cold, as desired.

Approximate Nutritional Information Per Serving

350 calories, 11g protein, 55g carbohydrates, 10g fat, 170mg cholesterol, 190mg sodium

Estimated Prep Time: . . . .*10 minutes*
Estimated Cooking Time: . . . .*10 minutes*
Total: . . . .*20 minutes*

CHOCOLATE MOUSSE CHEESECAKE

A chocolate lover's delight! Top with cherry pie filling or fresh strawberries for an extra special dessert.

Serves 6

Ingredients

1/2 cup chocolate water crumbs
1 pinch ground cinnamon
8 (1 ounce) squares semisweet chocolate
1 tablespoon butter
2 (8 ounce) packages cream cheese, softened
1 cup heavy whipping cream
1 teaspoon vanilla extract
2/3 cup white sugar
2 eggs, beaten
1 1/2 tablespoons unsweetened cocoa powder
1 1/2 cups water
Fresh sliced strawberries, as garnish (optional)*

Directions

Grease an 8-inch spring form pan that will fit inside the pressure cooker. Mix chocolate water crumbs and cinnamon together. Sprinkle on the bottom of spring form pan, pressing gently. Melt chocolate and butter together over a double boiler and set aside. Process cream cheese in food processor or electric mixer until smooth. Add chocolate mixture and process until well mixed. Add cream, vanilla extract, sugar and eggs, then cocoa powder until all ingredients are well incorporated. Pour mixture over crumbs in pan. Cover cake with piece of waxed paper and then cover entire pan with aluminum foil. Add water to pressure cooker. Place pan on a trivet in pressure cooker. Close lid; bring up to high pressure, then lower heat and pressure cook 45-50 minutes. Remove cooker from heat and let pressure drop naturally. Remove cheesecake from cooker, and let cool to room temperature. Remove cheesecake from pan, and refrigerate for 8 hours before serving.

Approximate Nutritional Information Per Serving

480 calories, 8g protein, 33g carbohydrates, 36g fat, 160mg cholesterol, 310mg sodium
*not included in nutritional analysis

Estimated Prep Time: . . . .*15 minutes*
Estimated Cooking Time: . . . .*50 minutes*
Total: . . . .*1 h 5 minutes*

PINEAPPLE COMPOTE WITH ICE CREAM

This wonderful tropical dessert is perfect on a long summer day. You can also make your own variations of this compote by using different fruits, such as strawberries or peaches.

Serves 6

Ingredients

3 tablespoons butter
4 tablespoons brown sugar
3 cups crushed pineapple w/juice
3 tablespoons dark rum (or more to liking)
1/4 teaspoon vanilla extract
1 teaspoon cinnamon
1 quart vanilla ice cream

Directions

Melt butter in the pressure cooker and then add the sugar. Stir. Add the pineapple with juice (juice should be 1/2 cup -if not add enough water to amount of 1/2 cup), rum, extract and cinnamon.

Close lid; bring to high pressure, then lower heat and pressure cook for 3 minutes.

Release pressure with the automatic release method, open lid and stir. Serve warm over vanilla ice cream.

Approximate Nutritional Information Per Serving

320 calories, 4g protein, 44g carbohydrates, 14g fat, 50mg cholesterol, 75mg sodium

Estimated Prep Time: . . . . .0 minutes
Estimated Cooking Time: . . . . .3 minutes
Total: . . . . .3 minutes

APPLE RAISIN BREAD PUDDING

This bread pudding is very versatile and has a lovely texture. Try adding a pinch of nutmeg and mace to produce a sumptuous holiday dessert. Otherwise, enjoy this just as it is with a dollop of whipped cream.

Serves 8

Ingredients

2 tablespoons butter
2 cups chopped cored cooking apples (about 2 medium)
3 cups day-old bread cubes (about 3 slices)
1/2 cup raisins
4 eggs
2 cups skim or low-fat milk
1/3 cup firmly packed brown sugar
1 teaspoon vanilla
3/4 teaspoon pumpkin pie spice
Whipped cream or vanilla ice cream (optional)
Apple wedges (optional)

Directions

In pressure cooker, melt the butter. Stir in chopped apples. Close lid, bring to high pressure, then lower heat and cook for 3 minutes. Release pressure with the cold water release method, open lid and add bread cubes and raisins.

In a medium bowl, beat together eggs, milk, sugar, vanilla and spice until sugar is dissolved. Add in apple mixture and stir. Cover and refrigerate several hours or overnight.

In 1 1/2 quart casserole dish, bake mixture in preheated 350° F. oven until knife inserted near center comes out clean, t about 45-55 minutes.

Serve hot, warm or chilled, garnished with either whipped cream, Ice cream and/or apple wedges, if desired.

Approximate Nutritional Information Per Serving

200 calories, 7g protein, 31g carbohydrates, 6g fat, 115mg cholesterol, 150mg sodium

Estimated Prep Time: . . . . .5 minutes
Estimated Cooking Time: . . . . .60 minutes
Total: . . . . .1 h 5 minutes

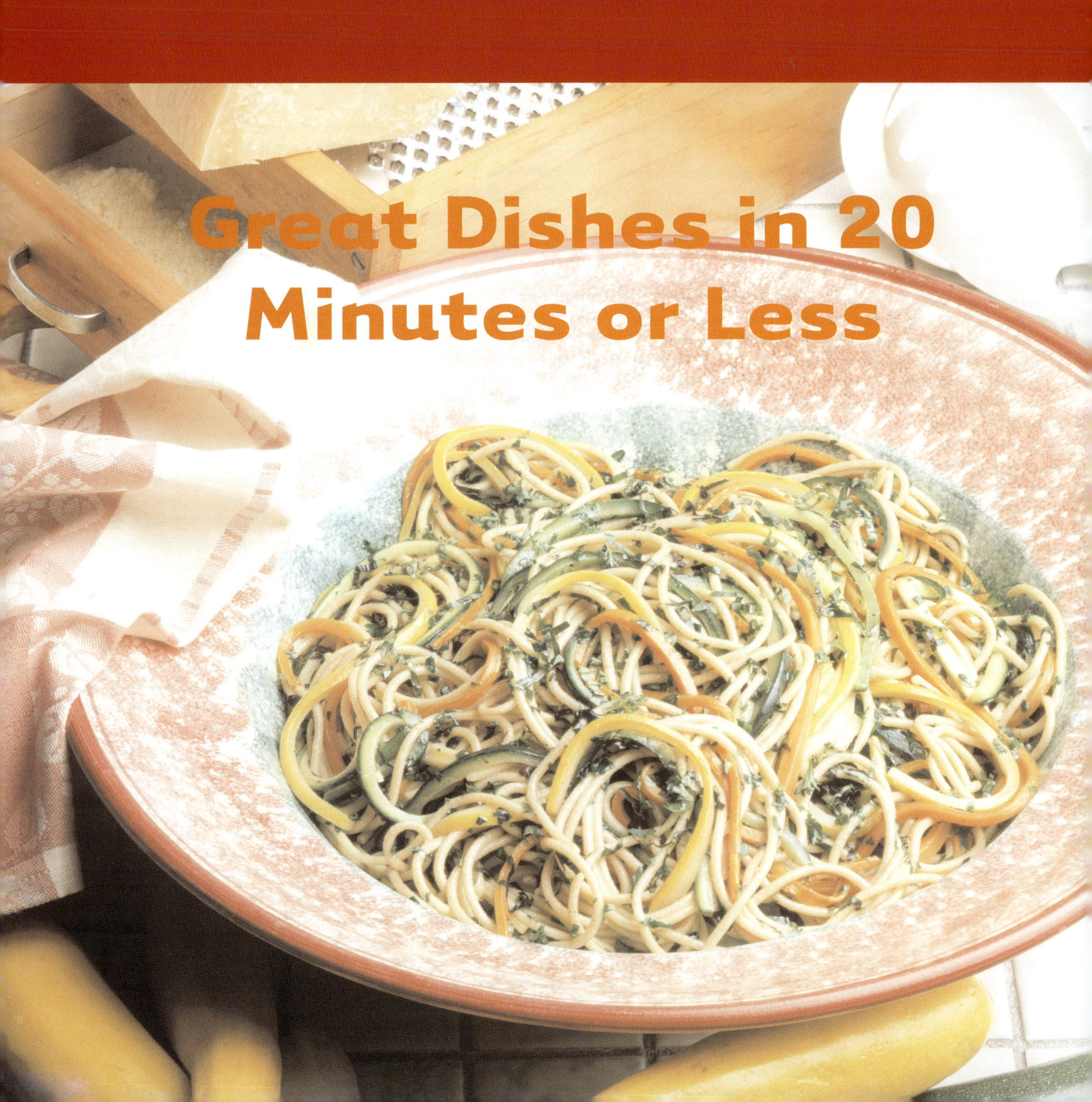

Great Dishes in 20 Minutes or Less

INDIAN SUMMER STEW

Satisfying and spicy, this stew is perfect for the warm weather of summer.

Serves 6

Ingredients

    2 tablespoons olive oil
    1 medium yellow onion, chopped
    1 medium green pepper, chopped
    3 medium zucchinis cut into 1/4" slices
    2 cups frozen corn
    1 teaspoon diced jalapeno
    2 breasts of chicken, cut into 1" cubes
    2 cups water
    1/2 teaspoon cumin
    8 ounces sour cream
    1 diced red pepper
    Salt and pepper to taste*

Directions

Warm oil in cooker. Add onions and garlic and sauté on medium- high heat until opaque. Add chicken and brown lightly. Add remaining ingredients, except sour cream and diced red pepper.

Close lid, bring to high pressure, then lower heat and cook for 5 minutes. Release pressure with the automatic release method. Add salt and pepper to taste. Serve in attractive bowls with sour cream and diced red pepper sprinkled on top.

Approximate Nutritional Information Per Serving

330 calories, 18g protein, 27g carbohydrates, 19g fat, 55mg cholesterol, 60mg sodium
*not included in nutritional value

    Estimated Prep Time: . . . . .10 minutes
    Estimated Cooking Time: . . . . .10 minutes
    Total: . . . . .20 minutes

BRAISED VEAL WITH CARROTS

This is a very tender and succulent veal dish in a rich Marsala wine sauce.

Serves 6

Ingredients

    4 tablespoons olive oil
    2 large onions, quartered
    1 clove garlic, minced
    1 tablespoon chopped fresh rosemary
    2 pounds cubed veal for stew
    1 cup Marsala or other sweet wine
    1 pound carrots, peeled and grated
    1 1/2 cups beef broth
    Freshly ground pepper to taste*

Directions

Warm 2 tablespoons of olive oil in pressure cooker pot over low heat. Add the onions, garlic and rosemary and sauté until tender and translucent, about 8 minutes. Remove from cooker and set aside in bowl.

In cooker, warm the remaining 2 tablespoons of olive oil over high heat. Add the meat and brown well on all sides, sprinkling a little salt after it has browned. Add the wine and let it bubble up. Add the sautéed onions, the butternut squash, and the broth to cover.

Close lid, bring to high pressure, then lower heat and cook for 10 minutes.

Release pressure with the automatic release method, open lid and season with salt and pepper before serving.

Approximate Nutritional Information Per Serving

360 calories, 33g protein, 17g carbohydrates, 13g fat, 125mg cholesterol, 410mg sodium
*not included in nutritional analysis

    Estimated Prep Time: . . . . .2 minutes
    Estimated Cooking Time: . . . . .18 minutes
    Total: . . . . .20 minutes

CHICKEN BREASTS WITH LEEKS AND MUSHROOMS

Sautéed chicken breasts unite with a tangy red wine sauce to create this magnificent entrée. Serve this dish with steamed rice.

Serves 8

Ingredients

1 cup flour
1 teaspoon paprika
1/2 teaspoon salt
1/2 teaspoon pepper
1 whole chicken fryer (about 3 pounds), cut into pieces
4 tablespoons olive oil
White part of 4 leeks, sliced, washed well, and patted dry
24 mushrooms, sliced
1 cup dry red wine
1 cup chicken broth
2 teaspoons dried thyme, crumbled
32 Kalamata or other brine-cured black olives, pitted and chopped
1 teaspoon drained bottled capers, chopped
Fresh lemon juice to taste

Directions

In a shallow bowl, mix together flour, paprika, salt and pepper. Dredge the chicken parts into the flour mixture, shaking off excess.

In pressure cooker, sauté the chicken in oil, turning once, until golden brown. Reduce heat to moderately low and stir in the leeks, mushrooms, wine, broth and thyme. Close lid; bring to high pressure, then lower heat and cook mixture for 9 minutes.

Release pressure using the cold-water release method, open lid and transfer chicken and leek mixture to a platter. Add the olives, capers and lemon juice to pressure cooker and cook the mixture, stirring, for 1 minute. Serve the chicken topped with the olive mixture.

Approximate Nutritional Information Per Serving

590 calories, 36g protein, 23g carbohydrates, 37g fat, 130mg cholesterol, 660mg sodium

Estimated Prep Time: . . . .*5 minutes*
Estimated Cooking Time: . . . .*15 minutes*
Total: . . . .*20 minutes*

CURRIED CHICKEN SALAD WITH BROCCOLLI

This chicken salad has an amazing flavor! The blend of the sour cream, mayonnaise and buttermilk give an exceptional zest to this salad.

Serves 7

Ingredients

3 cups water
2 tablespoons lemon juice
1 bay leaf
1 clove garlic, halved
12 black peppercorns
1 pound skinned, boned chicken breasts
7 cups small fresh broccoli florets
3/4 cup chopped red bell pepper
1/2 cup nonfat buttermilk
1/3 cup nonfat sour cream
1/3 cup nonfat mayonnaise
1 teaspoon curry powder
1/2 teaspoon salt
1/8 teaspoon coarsely ground pepper

Directions

Combine water, lemon juice, bay leaf, garlic and peppercorns in a pressure cooker pot; bring to a boil. Reduce heat and add chicken. Close lid, bring to high pressure, then lower heat and cook for 6 minutes. Release pressure with the automatic release method, remove chicken from pot and let cool. Discard cooking liquid. Shred chicken into bite-sized pieces; set aside.

Place broccoli into pressure cooker and add 1/2 cup water. Close lid, bring to high pressure, then lower heat and cook for 1 minute. Release pressure using cold-water release method according to manufacturer's directions. Combine chicken, broccoli, and red bell pepper in bowl. Combine buttermilk and sour cream, mayonnaise, curry powder, salt and pepper in a bowl. Add to chicken mixture, tossing gently to coat. Refrigerate before serving.

Approximate Nutritional Information Per Serving

130 calories, 19g protein, 10g carbohydrates, 1.5g fat, 40mg cholesterol, 320mg sodium

Estimated Prep Time: . . . .*10 minutes*
Estimated Cooking Time: . . . .*7 minutes*
Total: . . . .*17 minutes*

LOBSTER RISOTTO

Use the freshest lobster meat available to achieve maximum flavor for the risotto. Serve this satisfying rice as an entrée or a side dish.

4 Servings

Ingredients

3 tablespoons unsalted butter
I small onion, finely chopped
I cup Arborio (short-grain) rice
1/4 cup dry white wine
2 cups low sodium chicken stock
1 medium tomato, peeled, seeded and diced
1/3 cup Parmesan cheese
1/2 cup lobster meat
Freshly ground pepper, to taste*
Basil, as garnish*

Directions

Heat two tablespoons of unsalted butter in pressure cooker over medium heat. Add onion and sauté until translucent. Stir frequently to prevent browning. Add rice and sauté 3 minutes. Add wine and cook, stirring, for one minute. Add chicken stock, tomatoes and lobster meat.

Close the cooker and bring to high pressure. Lower heat and cook for 7 minutes. Remove from heat and release with the automatic release method. Open lid.

Stir in remaining one tablespoon of butter and add Parmesan cheese. Season with pepper and basil. Stir thoroughly until all ingredients are blended.

Approximate Nutritional Information Per Serving

350 calories, 14g protein, 55g carbohydrates, 13g fat, 55g cholesterol, 420mg sodium
*not included in nutritional analysis

Estimated Prep Time: . . . . .5 minutes
Estimated Cooking Time: . . . . .15 minutes
Total: . . . . .20 minutes

MEXICAN BLACK BEAN CHILI

Chili pepper packs less heat than fresh chipolte peppers to, so if you're not a big fan of hot dishes, opt for this alternative without sacrificing any flavor

Serves 8

Ingredients

1 1/2 cup black beans, rinsed and quick soaked*
4 cups water
2 lbs butternut squash, washed, peeled, seeded, and cut into 8 pieces
1 large yam, peeled, & cut into 6 pieces
4 garlic cloves, peeled and minced
2-3 canned chipolte peppers
1 tablespoon olive oil

Condiments:

1 red pepper (diced)
1 large tomato (diced)
Sour cream or plain yogurt
1 ripe avocado (peeled, pitted & sliced) 1 small onion (diced)
6 tablespoons chopped cilantro 2 limes, cut into wedges

Directions

Heat olive oil in pressure cooker on medium-high heat. Add garlic and chipoltes and saute 30 seconds. Add squash, yam and beans, along with soaking liquid. Stir well. Close lid, bring to high pressure, then lower heat on stove and cook for 15 minutes. Release the pressure using cold-water release. Discard chipoltes. Mash the beans, yam and squash by pressing them against the side of the pot with the back of a spoon. Serve in large soup bowls and allow guests to add condiments.

*To quick soak the beans:

Place the rinsed beans in the steamer basket on top of steamer trivet and put inside the pressure cooker. Add 6 cups of water. Close lid, bring to high pressure and cook for 2 minutes. Release pressure using the cold water release method. Remove beans and rinse again. Your beans are now ready to be cooked.

Approximate Nutritional Information Per Serving

260 calories, 10g protein, 43g carbohydrates, 8g fat, 5mg cholesterol, 240mg sodium

Estimated Prep Time: . . . . .5 minutes
Estimated Cooking Time: . . . . .15 minutes
Total: . . . . .20 minutes

PASTA WITH SCALLOPS, ZUCCHINI AND TOMATOES

This pasta dish is light and refreshing and perfect for a warm summer day.
Serves 6

Ingredients
1 pound fettuccine pasta, cooked
1/4 cup olive oil
3 cloves garlic, minced
2 zucchinis, diced
1/2 teaspoon salt
1/2 teaspoon crushed red pepper flakes
4 Roma tomatoes, chopped
1 pound bay scallops
1 cup chopped fresh basil
1 cup tomato sauce
2 tablespoons grated Parmesan cheese

Directions
In pressure cooker, heat olive oil, add garlic and cook until tender. Add zucchini, salt, red pepper flakes, chopped tomatoes, bay scallops, fresh basil and tomato sauce. Close lid, bring to high pressure, then lower heat on stove and pressure cook for 2 minutes.

Release pressure using the automatic release method, open lid and pour sauce over cooked pasta and serve with grated Parmesan cheese.

Approximate Nutritional Information Per Serving
440 calories, 26g protein, 57g carbohydrates, 13g fat, 25mg cholesterol, 750mg sodium

Estimated Prep Time: . . . . .5 minutes
Estimated Cooking Time: . . . . .2 minutes
Total: .7 minutes

MARMITAKO (FRESH TUNA, POTATO AND GREEN PEPPER, BASQUE STYLE)

This recipe comes from the northern area of Spain and is quick and easy to make.
Serves 6

Ingredients
2 tablespoons olive oil
1 medium onion, chopped
1 green bell pepper, cut into strips
3 large baking potatoes, peeled and cut into bite-sized chunks
2 tablespoons paprika
3 cups water
1 pound fresh tuna, cut into small chunks
1 teaspoon kosher salt

Directions
Heat the olive oil over medium heat in the pressure cooker. Add the onion and sauté for about 3 minutes, just until it begins to soften. Add the green pepper and cook for another 3 minutes. Add the potatoes and paprika; mix well. Cover with 3 cups water.

Close lid and bring to high pressure. Lower the heat, stabilizing the pressure and cook for 6 minutes.

Release the pressure using the cold-water release method. Open the cooker.

Salt the tuna and add it to the pressure cooker. Over medium-high heat, cook for 2 more minutes, stirring well until the tuna is opaque but not overcooked. Serve in bowls.

Approximate Nutritional Information Per Serving
270 calories, 25g protein, 21g carbohydrates, 10g fat, 35mg cholesterol, 430mg sodium

Estimated Prep Time: . . . . .5 minutes
Estimated Cooking Time: . . . . .15 minutes
Total: .20 minutes

COQ AU VIN

This is a French chicken dish cooked with vegetables, herbs and red wine and is absolutely marvelous. Make it for special occasions and you will be sure to receive plenty of compliments. Serve with hot cooked noodles, crusty French bread and a green salad, if desired.

Serves 4

Ingredients
1 cup dry red wine
3 lb. boneless chicken, cut in serving pieces
1/2 teaspoon thyme
Flour for dusting
2 tablespoons minced parsley
1 tablespoon olive oil
1 bay leaf
3 slices bacon, minced
1/8 teaspoon salt
1 large onion, chopped
1/8 teaspoon pepper
2 cloves garlic, minced
1/4 pound fresh mushrooms, cleaned and sliced
1 carrot, scraped and diced
1 tablespoon flour

Directions
Dust the chicken parts with flour. Heat the oil in the cooker until very hot and brown as many chicken pieces as will comfortably fit at one time. Remove the chicken to a warm platter. Add the bacon, onion, garlic and carrot to the cooker and sauté until the onion is wilted. Stir in the tablespoon of flour, then gradually add the wine and stir until thickened and smooth. Add the thyme, parsley, bay leaf, salt and pepper, and then return the chicken to the cooker. Close the lid and bring to high pressure, then lower heat and cook for 8 minutes. Release the pressure with the automatic release method and remove the lid. Add the mushrooms and simmer, uncovered, 3 minutes. Discard the bay leaf. Serve.

Approximate Nutritional Information Per Serving
410 calories, 32g protein, 10g carbohydrates, 24g fat, 105mg cholesterol, 230mg sodium

Estimated Prep Time: . . . .*5 minutes*
Estimated Cooking Time: . . . .*15 minutes*
Total: . . . .*20 minutes*

OPEN SESAME SAVORY CHICKEN

Asian flavors and aromas make this dish exciting and unique. Try serving this with Asian cellophane noodles.

Serves 4

Ingredients
2 1/2 pounds chicken thighs, skinless and boneless
2 tablespoons canola oil
2 teaspoons sugar
1 tablespoon sesame oil (available at Asian stores)
1/4 cup Hoisin sauce (available at Asian grocery stores)
1 1/2 cups apple cider
1 cup sliced ripe star fruits
1 1/2 cups pitted prunes
Crushed red pepper flakes to taste*
Salt and ground black pepper to taste*

Directions
Trim any remaining fat from chicken. In large pressure cooker, heat oil over medium high heat. Add chicken and cook until browned. Remove chicken.

Combine sugar, sesame oil, and hoisin sauce in a bowl, mix well and add to the chicken. Blend well. Add cider, star fruits, prunes, red pepper flakes, salt and pepper to chicken.

Close lid, bring to high pressure, then lower heat and cook for 10 minutes. Remove from heat and use automatic release method to remove the pressure.

Arrange chicken on serving platter. Garnish and serve hot.

Approximate Nutritional Information Per Serving
420 calories, 6g protein, 78g carbohydrates, 12g fat, 15mg cholesterol, 270mg sodium
*not included in nutritional analysis

Estimated Prep Time: . . . .*0 minutes*
Estimated Cooking Time: . . . .*20 minutes*
Total: . . . .*20 minutes*

QUICK AND EASY STEAK STEW

A fast and easy stew for those cold nights when you want comfort food, but don't want to spend a lot of time cooking.

Serves 4

Ingredients
1 pound round steak, cut into bite size pieces
4 medium potatoes, cut in _" cubes
4 carrots, sliced _" thick
1 medium onion, coarsely chopped
1 can Campbell's Golden Mushroom Soup
2 cans water
1 teaspoon salt
2 tablespoons canola oil
3 tablespoons corn starch

Directions
Heat canola oil on medium-high heat in the cooker and brown steak cubes. Add the onions and stir for one minute. Add vegetables, soup, salt and two soup cans full of water.

Close lid, bring to high pressure, then lower heat and cook for 4 minutes. Release pressure using cold-water release method.

Thicken with cornstarch dissolved in water. Serve hot.

Approximate Nutritional Information Per Serving
430 calories, 31g protein, 47g carbohydrates, 13g fat, 75mg cholesterol, 1130mg sodium

Estimated Prep Time: . . . . .10 minutes
Estimated Cooking Time: . . . . .7 minutes
Total: . . . . .17 minutes

SHRIMP FEAST

Enjoy this one-pot shrimp feast for easy, summertime entertaining!
Serves 4

Ingredients
4 large potatoes, peeled and quartered
2 or 3 medium onions, quartered
1 dozen large shrimp
Old Bay Seasoning

Directions
Place potatoes and onions in the pressure cooker, close lid and bring up to high pressure, then lower heat and cook for 5 minutes.

Release the pressure using the cold-water method. Open the cooker, add the shrimp and cook uncovered for 2 minutes.

Sprinkle all with Old Bay seasoning and serve.

Approximate Nutritional Information Per Serving
160 calories, 7g protein, 32g carbohydrates, 0.5g fat, 30mg cholesterol, 40mg sodium

Estimated Prep Time: . . . . .5 minutes
Estimated Cooking Time: . . . . .7 minutes
Total: . . . . .12 minutes

Home Canning

HOME CANNING OVERVIEW:

Home canning is a method of preserving food that provides us with a gratifying method for producing some of our favorite recipes. Canning our recipes enable us to store them and enjoy for ourselves or give as gifts to friends & loved ones. Understanding the basic steps for preparation and right equipment are all you need to create a fabulous array of provisions to stock in your pantry. Once the method has been mastered, most people find that canning is one of the most simple and rewarding ways to ensure having your favorite fruits, vegetables, and even meats year-round.

Although canning food at home has traditionally been associated with pastoral residents, it has now begun to emerge as a new trend in greater populated areas. Families in suburban towns as well as urban dwellers are educating themselves on the methods of canning. These basic guidelines will allow you to learn how to can your most favorite recipes with pride.

WHY CAN FOODS?

Canning can be a safe and cost-effective way to preserve quality food at home. It is an important, safe method of food preservation if practiced properly. The canning process involves placing foods in jars and heating them to a temperature which destroys microorganisms that could be a health hazard or cause the food to spoil. Air is driven from the jar during heating, and as it cools, a vacuum seal is formed. The vacuum seal prevents air from getting back into the product, protecting it from microorganisms that could recontaminate the food.

Before You Begin: Basic Equipment for Canning
- Pressure Canner or Water Bath canner with wire basket (depending on the recipe)
- Jar lifter
- Ladle
- Colander
- Spatula or bubble freer
- Timer
- Jar Wrench
- Lid Wand
- Wire strainer
- Cooking thermometer
- Wide mouth funnel
- Glass Jars—Use only standard home canning jars. Also commonly referred to as 'Mason Jars'
- Canning Lids—these flat metal lids with sealing compound and a metal screw band are the most popular type of lid for home-canned products.

JAR SELECTION, PREPARATION AND USE:

Examine jars and discard those with nicks, cracks and rough edges. These defects will not permit an airtight seal on the jar, and food spoilage will result. All canning jars should be washed in soapy water, rinsed well and then kept hot before use. This could be done in the dishwasher or by placing the jars in the water that is heating in your canner. The jars need to be kept hot to prevent breakage when they're filled with a hot product and placed in the canner for processing.

Jars processed in a boiling water bath canner for 10 minutes or more or in a pressure cooker will be sterilized during processing. Jars that will be filled with food and processed for less than 10 minutes in a boiling water bath canner need to be sterilized by boiling them for 10 minutes. NOTE: If you are at an altitude of 1000 feet or more, boil an additional minute for each 1000 feet of additional altitude. See below for canning methods and recipe timing.

LID SELECTION, PREPARATION & USE

The common self-sealing lid consists of a flat metal lid held in place by a metal screw band during processing. The flat lid is crimped around its bottom edge to form a trough, which is filled with a colored gasket material. When jars are processed, the lid gasket softens and flows slightly to cover the jar-sealing surface, yet allows air to escape from the jar.

It is best to buy only the quantity of lids you will use in a year. Never reuse lids. To ensure a good seal, carefully follow the manufacturer's directions in preparing lids for use. Examine all metal lids carefully. Do not use old, dented, or deformed lids or lids with gaps or other defects in the sealing gasket.

Follow the manufacturer's guidelines enclosed with or on the box for tightening the jar lids properly.
• If screw bands are too tight, air cannot vent during processing, and food will discolor during storage.
• Over-tightening also may cause lids to buckle and jars to break, especially with pressure-processed food.
• If screw bands are too loose, liquid may escape from jars during processing, seals may fail, and the food will need to be reprocessed.

Do not retighten lids after processing jars. As jars cool, the contents in the jar contract, pulling the self-sealing lid firmly against the jar to form a high vacuum.

Screw bands are not needed on stored jars. They can be removed easily after jars are cooled. When removed, washed, dried, and stored in a dry area, screw bands may be used many times. If left on stored jars, they become difficult to remove, often rust, and may not work properly again.

CANNING METHODS:

There are two safe ways of canning, depending on the type of food being canned. These are the pressure canning method and the boiling water bath method.

PRESSURE CANNING METHOD:

Pressure canning is the only safe method of canning low-acid foods (those with a ph of more than 4.6). Pressure canning is necessary in low-acid foods. Low-acid foods include all vegetables, meats, poultry and seafood. This method is also necessary for canning such items as soups, stews and chili.

Jars of food are placed in 2 to 3 inches of water in a pressure cooker and heated to a temperature of at least 240 °F or above for the correct length of time. Note: This temperature can only be reached in a pressure cooker/canner. Never attempt to can low-acid foods using the water bath method.

STEPS FOR PRESSURE CANNER METHOD

Place 2 to 3 inches of water in the cooker. Keep jars, lids and rings lids in very hot water until time to use. Fill clean, hot jars one at a time. Allow proper headspace detailed in recipe to allow for expansion, use a bubble freer or narrow spatula between the food and the side of the jar to release any air bubbles. With a clean, damp cloth, wipe jar rims and put on lids.

PROCESSING INSTRUCTIONS:

Fill the jars. Allow the proper headspace according to processing directions for specific foods. This is necessary so that all the extra air will be removed during processing, and a tight vacuum seal will be formed.

To make sure that air bubbles have not been trapped inside the jar, run a bubble freer or any plastic or rubber-like utensil around the edges of the jar, gently shifting the food, so that any trapped air is released. After the air bubbles have been removed, more liquid may need to be added to the jar to ensure proper headspace.

Wipe off the rims of the jars with a clean, damp cloth.
Screw on the lids, but not too tightly — air needs to escape during processing.
Set the jars of food on the rack in the canner so steam can flow around each jar. Add more boiling water or take out some as needed so that the water is at least 1 inch over the tops of the jars. (If you add more water, pour it between the jars, not directly on them, to prevent breakage.) Put the lid on the cooker.

Keep the pressure constant by regulating the heat under the canner. Do not lower the pressure by opening the vent or lifting the weight.
Keep drafts from blowing on the canner. Fluctuating pressure causes loss of liquid from jars and under-processing.
When the processing is completed, carefully remove the canner from the heat. If the canner is too heavy, simply turn it off.
Let the pressure in the canner drop to zero using the natural release method. Do not use the cold water pressure release method for pressure canning. Never open the vent to hasten the reduction in pressure when canning foods.
When the canner is depressurized, open the vent. Wait an additional two minutes and then open the canner.
Unfasten the lid, and tilt the far side up, so the steam escapes away from you. Do not leave the canner unopened, or the food inside could begin to spoil. Use a jar lifter to carefully remove the jars from the canner. Place the hot jars on a rack, dry towels, boards or newspaper, right side up to prevent the jars from breaking on contact with a cold surface. Leave at least 1 inch of space between the jars.
Do not tighten the lids. Allow the jars to cool, untouched for 12 to 24 hours.

BOILING WATER BATH METHOD:

The boiling water bath method is safe for fruits, and pickles as well as pie filling, jams, jellies, marmalade and other preserves. In this method, jars of food are heated by being completely covered with boiling water (212 °F at sea level).

High-acid foods contain enough acid (ph of 4.6 or less) so that the Clostridium Botulinum (Botulism) spores can't grow and produce deadly toxins. High-acid foods include fruits and properly pickled vegetables. These foods can be safely canned at boiling temperatures in a water bath.

Although they are considered fruit, tomatoes have ph values close to 4.6. Therefore you should typically process them in a pressure canner.

STEPS FOR BOILING WATER BATH METHOD

Fill the canner about halfway with hot water. Turn on the burner and heat the water.

Have the water in the canner hot but not boiling to prevent breakage of the jars when they're placed in the canner.

Follow the same steps detailed in the pressure canner method for filling jars.

When the water in the canner reaches a rolling boil, begin counting the correct processing time. Boil gently and steadily for the recommended time, adjusting the heat and adding more boiling water as necessary.

Use a jar lifter to carefully remove the jars as soon as the processing time is up. Place the hot jars right side up on a rack, dry towels, boards or newspapers to prevent the jars from breaking on contact with a cold surface. Leave at least 1 inch of space between jars.

Do not tighten the lids

Allow the jars to cool untouched for 12 to 14 hours.

SELECTING THE CORRECT PROCESSING TIME

To destroy microorganisms in low-acid foods processed with a pressure cooker, you must:
- Process the jars for the correct number of minutes at suggested setting (low or high pressure)
- Allow cooker to cool at room temperature until it is completely depressurized.

To destroy microorganisms in high-acid foods processed in a boiling-water bath, you must:
- Process jars for the correct number of minutes in boiling water.
- Cool the jars at room temperature.

The food may spoil if you fail to use the proper processing times, fail to vent steam from canners properly, process at lower pressure than specified, process for fewer minutes than specified, or cool the pressure cooker with water.

FINISHING TOUCHES:

Testing the Lid for a Proper Seal:

Most two-piece lids will seal with a "pop" sound while they're cooling. When it is completely cool, test the lid. It should be curved downward and should not move when pressed with a finger. If a jar is not sealed, refrigerate it and use the unspoiled food within two to three days or freeze it.

If liquid has been lost from sealed jars do not open them to replace it, simply plan to use these first. The food may discolor, but if sealed, the food is safe.

Unsealed Jars: What to Do

If a lid fails to seal, you must reprocess within 24 hours. Remove the lid, and check the jar-sealing surface for tiny nicks. If necessary, change the jar. Always use a new, properly prepared lid, and reprocess using the same processing time. The quality of reprocessed food is poor.

Instead of reprocessing, unsealed jars of food also can be frozen. Transfer food to a freezer-safe container and freeze. Single, unsealed jars can be refrigerated and used within several days.

Always Inspect Canned Food Before Consuming:

Just as you would avoid a foul smelling, leaking or opened jar of food at the supermarket, don't taste or use home canned food that shows any sign of spoilage. Examine all jars before opening them. A bulging lid or leaking jar is almost always a sure sign of spoilage. When you open the jar, look for other signs such as spurting liquid, unusual odor or mold.

STERILIZATION OF EMPTY JARS

Use sterile jars for all boiling water bath recipes. To sterilize empty jars, put them right side up on the rack in a boiling-water bath. Fill the bath and jars with hot (not boiling) water to 1 inch above the tops of the jars. Boil 10 minutes. Remove and drain hot sterilized jars one at a time. Save the hot water for processing filled jars. Fill jars with food, add lids, and tighten screw bands.

Empty jars used for vegetables, meats, and fruits to be processed in a pressure canner need not be sterilized beforehand. It is also unnecessary to sterilize jars for fruits, tomatoes, and pickled or fermented foods that will be processed 10 minutes or longer in a boiling-water canner.

Label and Store Jars:

The screw bands should be removed from the sealed jars to prevent them from rusting on. The screw bands should then be washed, dried and stored for later use.

Store in a clean, cool, dark, dry place. The best temperature is between 50 and 70 °F. Avoid storing canned foods in a warm place near hot pipes, a range or a furnace, or in direct sunlight. They lose quality in a few weeks or months, depending on the temperature and may even spoil. Keep canned goods dry. Dampness may corrode metal lids and cause leakage so food will spoil. For best quality, use canned foods within one year.

Pressure Canning
Recipes

PASTA SAUCE

Servings: 32 - 8oz servings
Yields: 4 pints
Headspace: 1 inch
Time: 20 minutes / low pressure setting

Ingredients

- 15 lbs tomatoes cored and chopped
- 2 tablespoons olive oil
- 3/4 cup peeled, chopped onion
- 4 garlic cloves, peeled and minced
- 1/2 pound mushrooms, chopped
- 1/4 cup fresh parsley, chopped
- 3 tablespoons salt
- 2 bay leaves
- 2 teaspoons oregano
- 1 teaspoon black pepper
- 1/4 cup brown sugar

Directions

Place tomatoes in large saucepan and boil for 25 minutes uncovered. Allow cooling slightly then running through a food mill or sieving to remove skins and seeds.

In a large skillet, heat olive oil and sauté onions, garlic and mushrooms until tender. Place the sautéed vegetables in a stockpot, add tomatoes and remainder of ingredients and bring to a boil. Lower heat and simmer, uncovered for approx 25 minutes, stirring frequently to avoid burning. Ladle into Jars. Follow pressure cooker method- steps for canning. Process for 20 minutes / low pressure setting.

Approximate Nutritional Information Per Serving

60 calories, 2g protein, 12g carbohydrate, 670mg sodium, 1.5g fat.

Estimated Prep Time: . . . .*15 minutes*
Estimated Cooking Time: . . . .*45 minutes*
Total: *1hour*

SPICY CHILI SAUCE

Servings: 22-4tbsp servings
Yields: 4 pints
Headspace: 1/2 inch
Time: 35 minutes / low pressure setting

Ingredients

- 4 long green chili peppers
- 2 onions peeled and chopped
- 7 garlic cloves peeled and minced
- 4 tablespoons olive oil
- 5 tomatoes peeled cored and chopped
- 1/3 cup tomato paste
- 1/4 cup lemon juice
- 1 tablespoon grated lemon peel
- 1 1/2 teaspoons salt
- 1 teaspoon dried coriander
- Chili powder to taste

Directions

Place chili peppers on a baking sheet and broil for 30 minutes, turning occasionally to brown evenly. Remove from oven and allow to cool. Remove skins, stems and seeds. Puree them in a blender or food processor.

Sauté onions and garlic in the olive oil until tender. Combine onions, garlic and olive oil with Chili pepper puree in saucepan with remaining ingredients. Bring to a boil. Reduce heat and simmer for 15 minutes or until thick. Ladle into Jars. Follow pressure cooker method- steps for canning. Process for 35 minutes / low pressure setting

Approximate Nutritional Information Per Serving

40 calories, 1g protein, 4g carbohydrates, 160mg sodium, 2.5g fat

Estimated Prep Time: . . . .*30 minutes*
Estimated Cooking Time: . . . .*1 hour*
Total: *1h 30minutes*

BARBEQUE SAUCE

Servings: 55-2tbsp servings
Yields: 4 pints
Headspace: 1 inch
Time: 20 minutes / low pressure setting

Ingredients

1 cup peeled, chopped onions
3/4 cup chopped celery
1 tablespoon of salt
1 teaspoon paprika
2 tablespoons mustard
3 tablespoons Worcestershire sauce
1 1/2 cups tomato paste
1 1/2 cups ketchup
16 oz. Water
1/2 cup distilled white vinegar
1 1/2 cups brown sugar

DIRECTIONS

Combine all ingredients into a stockpot and bring to a boil. Lower heat and simmer for about 30 minutes, stirring constantly. Once sauce has thickened, ladle into jars. Follow pressure cooker method- steps for canning. Process for 20 minutes / low pressure setting.

Approximate Nutritional Information Per Serving

40 calories, 1g protein, 9g carbohydrates, 230mg sodium, 0g fat

Estimated Prep Time: . . . .*10 minutes*
Estimated Cooking Time: . . . .*50 minutes*
Total: *1hour*

SOUPS FOR ALL SEASONS VEGETABLE SOUP

Servings: 16-1cup servings
Yields: 4 pints
Headspace: 1 inch
Time: 95 minutes / low pressure setting

Ingredients

1 quart water or vegetable stock
8 tomatoes peeled cored and chopped
5 potatoes peeled and cut into cubes
3 cups lima beans (fresh or frozen)
5 cups corn kernels (fresh or frozen)
2 cups carrots peeled and sliced
1 cup chopped celery
1 1/2 cups peeled, chopped red onions
1/4 cup fresh minced parsley
2 bay leaves
Salt & Pepper to taste

Directions

Combine all ingredients in a large stockpot and bring to a boil. Cook over high heat for and additional 5 minutes. Ladle into jars. Follow pressure cooker method- steps for canning. Process for 95 minutes / low pressure setting.

Approximate Nutritional Information Per Serving

140 calories, 6g protein, 31g carbohydrates, 45mg sodium, 1g fat

Estimated Prep Time: . . . .*15 minutes*
Estimated Cooking Time: . . . .*95 minutes*
Total: *1h 50minutes*

SPLIT PEA SOUP

Servings: 8-1cup servings
Yields: 4 pints
Headspace: 1 inch
Time: 90 minutes / low pressure setting

Ingredients

2 pounds dry yellow split peas
3 1/2 quarts water
1/3 cup limejuice
2 cups peeled, chopped onions
3 3/4 cups peeled, sliced carrots
4 garlic cloves peeled and minced
1/2 tablespoon cumin seed
1/2 tablespoon coriander
1/2 tablespoon cayenne pepper
1 1/2 teaspoons salt

Directions

In a large stockpot, bring the split peas and water to a boil. Simmer gently, covered for about 1 hour or until peas have softened. Stir in remaining ingredients and continue to simmer for an additional 30 minutes. Check consistency and if necessary, thin with water. Ladle into jars. Follow pressure cooker method- steps for canning. Process for 90 minutes / low pressure setting.

Approximate Nutritional Information Per Serving

450 calories, 30g protein, 84g carbohydrates, 460mg sodium, 0g fat

Estimated Prep Time: ....*60 minutes*
Estimated Cooking Time: ....*120 minutes*
Total: *3hours*

BROCCOLI SOUP

Servings: 16-1cup servings
Yields: 4 pints
Headspace: 1 inch
Time: 40 minutes / low pressure setting

Ingredients

4 pounds broccoli whole
2 onions peeled and chopped
4 garlic cloves peeled and chopped
1/3 cup margarine or vegetable oil
3/4 cup uncooked white rice
15 cups vegetable or chicken broth
Tabasco sauce to taste
Salt & Pepper to taste

Directions

Cut broccoli florets from the stalks. Peel stalks and slice into 1-inch pieces. Sauté stalks, florets, onions and garlic in the margarine or vegetable oil. In a large saucepan combine the sautéed vegetables with rice and broth. Bring to a boil. Lower heat and simmer gently until vegetables are very soft. Puree soup in a blender, return to stockpot and add the Tabasco, salt and pepper. Bring to a boil. Cook for an additional 5 minutes. Ladle into jars. Follow pressure cooker method- steps for canning. Process for 40 minutes / low pressure setting.

Approximate Nutritional Information Per Serving

110 calories, 5g protein, 15g carbohydrates, 110mg sodium, 4.5g fat

Estimated Prep Time: ....*30 minutes*
Estimated Cooking Time: ....*40 minutes*
Total: ....*1h 10 minutes*

MIXED VEGETABLES

Servings: 33-1/2cup servings
Yields: 4 pints
Headspace: 1 inch
Time: 55 minutes / low pressure setting

Ingredients

- 5 cups sliced carrots
- 5 cups cut, whole kernel sweet corn
- 5 cups cut green beans
- 5 cups shelled lima beans
- 3 cups whole or crushed tomatoes
- 3 cups diced zucchini

Directions

Combine all vegetables in a large pot or kettle, and add enough water to cover pieces. Add 1teaspoon salt per quart to the jar, if desired. Boil 5 minutes. Ladle into jars (include the liquid). Leave 1inch headspace. Follow pressure cooker method- steps for canning. Process 55 minutes / low pressure setting.

Approximate Nutritional Information Per Serving

70 calories, 3g protein, 15g carbohydrates, 40mg sodium, 0g fat

Estimated Prep Time: . . . .*15 minutes*
Estimated Cooking Time: . . . .*55 minutes*
Total: . . . .*1h 10 minutes*

SPINACH AND OTHER GREENS

Servings: 40-1/2cup servings
Yields: 4 pints
Headspace: 1 inch
Time: 70 minutes / low pressure setting

Ingredients

- 10 pounds of Spinach or other leafy greens

Quality

Can only freshly harvested greens. Discard any wilted, discolored, diseased or insect-damaged leaves.Leaves should be tender and attractive in color.

Directions

Wash only small amounts of greens at one time. Drain water and continue rinsing until water is clear and free of grit. Cut out tough stems. Place 1 pound of greens at a time in basket and steam 3 to 5 minutes or until well wilted. Add 1/2 teaspoon of salt to each quart jar, if desired. Ladle into jars (include the liquid) Leave 1inch headspace. Follow pressure cooker method- steps for canning. Process 55 minutes / low pressure setting.

Approximate Nutritional Information Per Serving

25 calories, 3g protein, 4g carbohydrates, 105mg sodium, 0g fat

Estimated Prep Time: . . . .*15 minutes*
Estimated Cooking Time: . . . .*55 minutes*
Total: . . . .*1h 10 minutes*

CHILE CON CARNE

Servings: 8-1cup servings
Yields: 4 pints
Headspace: 1 inch
Time: 75 minutes / low pressure setting

Ingredients
1 1/2 cups dried red kidney beans
2 3/4 cups water
2 1/2 teaspoons salt
1 1/2 lbs ground beef
3/4 cup chopped onions
3/4 cup chopped peppers
1/2 teaspoon black pepper
2-5 tbsp chili powder
1 qt crushed tomatoes

Directions
Wash beans thoroughly and place them in a 2qt saucepan. Add cold water to a level of 2 – 3 inches above the beans and soak 12 to 18 hours. Drain and discard water. Combine beans with water and salt. Bring to a boil. Reduce heat and simmer for 30 minutes. Drain and discard water. In a separate skillet, brown ground beef, onions, and peppers.

Drain off fat and add to beans with remainder of ingredients. Simmer for an additional 5-10 minutes. Follow pressure cooker method- steps for canning. Process for 90 minutes / low pressure setting.

Approximate Nutritional Information Per Serving
300 calories, 26g protein, 28g carbohydrates, 590mg sodium, 11g fat

Estimated Prep Time: . . . . .30 minutes (plus soaking beans see recipe for details)
Estimated Cooking Time: . . . . .1h 40 minutes
Total: . . . . .2h 10 minutes

KING CRAB MEAT

Servings: 14-4oz servings
Yields: 4 pints
Headspace: 1 inch
Time: 70 minutes / low pressure setting

Ingredients
48 oz Crab Meat
Lemon Juice
Salt

Directions
Keep live crabs on ice until ready to can. Wash crabs thoroughly, using several changes of cold water. Simmer crabs 20 minutes in water containing 1/4 cup of lemon juice and 2 tablespoons of salt per gallon. Cool in cold water, drain, remove back shell, then remove meat from body and claws. Soak meat 2 minutes in cold water containing 2 cups of lemon juice and 2 tablespoons of salt (or up to 1 cup of salt, if desired) per gallon. Drain and squeeze meat to remove excess moisture. Fill jars with 12 ounces of crabmeat. Add 4 tablespoons of lemon juice per pint jar. Add hot water, leaving 1inch headspace. Follow pressure cooker method- steps for canning. Process for 70 minutes / low pressure setting.

Approximate Nutritional Information Per Serving
100 calories, 19g protein, 1g carbohydrates, 430mg sodium, 1.5g fat

Estimated Prep Time: . . . . .30 minutes
Estimated Cooking Time: . . . . .70 minutes
Total: . . . . .1h 10 minutes

General Questions & Troubleshooting

GENERAL QUESTIONS

How safe are Cooks Essentials pressure cookers? Will they explode like my mother's pressure cooker?

Cooks Essentials Pressure Cookers, which are U.L.-approved, are perfectly safe and do not explode. All our models contain three safety mechanisms that permit steam to escape when over pressurizing occurs. Unlike older models, the lids will not open until all the steam has dissipated and pressure has been completely released.

What's the difference between a high quality pressure cooker and a low-priced/low-quality pressure cooker?

Cooks Essentials pressure cookers are made of durable 18/10 stainless steel (not aluminum) with aluminum-clad bottoms and triple-lock safety systems. Each unit comes with an easy-to-understand instruction booklet and recipes. We also provide a 10-year warranty and a toll-free customer service number: 1-800-207-0806.

How do I use the steamer basket with the trivet?

Most Cooks Essentials pressure cookers come with a steamer basket (also known as a cooking rack) and a trivet. The basket is used for steaming foods without placing them directly into the cooking liquid. The steamer basket is especially good for steaming vegetables! The trivet is placed on the bottom of the cooker and the steamer basket is placed on top of it. This keeps the basket out of contact with any liquid.

How do I build pressure in my Cooks Essentials pressure cooker?

In order for the pressure cooker to build pressure, the cooking liquid in the pot has to be brought to a boil with the lid positioned and locked in place. As the cooking liquid begins to boil, steam is produced. The trapped steam will build up and compress, creating pressure. Therefore, once your cooker is loaded and locked into place, raise the burner heat to high*. As pressure builds, the pressure regulator valve will activate in accordance with the specifications and features of your pressure cooker.

There are three ways to know you have reached high pressure:

1. On pressure cookers with spring-mechanism valves, the pressure regulator valve will rise to indicate maximum pressure. On units with vent pipes, the developed weight valve will either begin to rock and move, or will rise up, depending on design.
2. You will notice a hissing sound coming from the pressure-regulator valve.
3. Steam will begin to escape from the spring-regulator valve—or in the case of pressure cooker with a developed weight valve, from the vent pipe.

Once you have reached high pressure, bring the burner heat to low. Depending on the design of your pressure cooker, you may notice a continuous or occasional low hissing sound as well as a slight sign of steam. Do not lower the burner heat too much, otherwise the internal temperature will drop and you will lose pressure in your cooker.

* *Electric stove owners should start out on a medium setting. Once high pressure is reached, move the pressure cooker to a different burner on a low heat setting.*

How do I release the pressure from my Cooks Essentials pressure cooker?

When the food has finished cooking, remove the pressure cooker the burner. Even though the pressure cooker is no longer on the heat source, the contents will continue to cook until the temperature and level of pressure drop.

There are three ways of releasing cooking pressure in a pressure cooker:

The Natural-Release Method:

Foods like stocks, tomato sauces, and certain cuts of meat benefit from continuing to cook in the pressure cooker as the pressure and temperature drop naturally after the unit is removed from the burner. The natural-release method can take anywhere from 10 minutes to over 20 minutes, depending on the kind of food in the pressure cooker and how much of it there is. You will know when the pressure has dropped completely once the spring-loaded pressure-regulator valve lowers completely or steam no longer comes out of the vent pie on the developed weight valve units.

The Cold-Water Release Method:

For the most part, you will want to lower and release the cooking pressure as quickly as possible in order to stop the cooking process. The quickest way to do this is to carefully take the pressure cooker from the stove and bring it to the sink. Place it in the sink in a tilted position, and allow a small amount of cold water to run over the lid of the cooker. This will stabilize the temperature and force the pressure to dissipate in a matter a seconds. You will normally hear a decompressing sound-almost like a swooshing "pop"-once all the pressure has been released.

The Automatic-Release Method:

Some of our pressure cooker models have an automatic release method, which enables you to release without having to place the pressure cooker under cold water. Consult the user's manual for your specific model to see if this is the case with your model. If so, you can use this method when preparing any recipes that call for the cold-release method.

Where can I find additional recipes for my Cooks Essentials pressure cooker?

Fagor America, Inc. offers a number of recipe books at a reasonable price, specifically designed for use with your Cooks Essentials pressure cooker. We also have some of our more popular recipes posted on our website at www.fagoramerica.com.

Do Cooks Essentials pressure cookers come with a warranty?

Your pressure cookers is backed by a lifetime warranty which guarantees it to be free from defects in material and workmanship for the entire life of the cooker, provided that the unit is used in accordance with the use and care instructions supplied, and for household use only. Moving and/or perishable parts, such as gaskets, internal component parts, etc. which are subject to normal wear and tear are excluded from the warranty. Also excluded are all defects resulting from accident, damaged suffered in transit, misuse or negligence (including overheating and boiling dry), normal wear and tear, such as scratched, dulling of the polish or staining, etc., and repairs or manipulations carried out by unauthorized or non-qualified personnel.

How do I contact a Customer Service Representative?

Customer Service Representatives are available to assist you Monday-Friday between the hours of 9am until 5pm EST. Our toll-free number is 1 (800) 207-0806. You can also email us 24 hours a day at info@fagoramerica.com.

TROUBLESHOOTING QUESTIONS

The lid of my pressure cooker is stuck!! How do I get it off?

There may still be a build up of pressure inside. Using the cold-water-release method, release any remaining pressure and try opening again. If you used the natural release method to depressurize the cooker, a slight vacuum may have developed. Heat the pressure cooker over high heat just until steam begins to come out of the pressure regulator valve. Using the cold-water-release method, release the pressure and try to open again.

Why doesn't my pressure cooker build up pressure?

There can be numerous reasons why pressure would not build up in your pressure cooker.

Reason: Not enough cooking liquid.
Solution: Always use a sufficient amount of cooking liquid for the type of food being prepared and the length of cooking. Consult the pressure-cooker recipe you are following for the amount of liquid.

Reason: The pressure cooker was not properly closed.
Solution: Refer to the instructional manual packaged with your cooker

Reason: The pressure cooker was not heated over high enough heat.
Solution: Always heat the closed pressure cooker over high heat until high pressure has been reached.

Reason: The rubber sealing gasket or ring is:
           Not in place- Always check to make sure that the rubber sealing gasket or ring is inserted

           Improperly positioned- Always check to see that the rubber sealing gasket or ring is properly inserted before using the pressure cooker each time

           Dirty- The rubber gasket or ring should be removed from the lid and washed after each use. Refer to your instruction manual for care and maintenance tips.

           Worn- After continued use, the rubber sealing gasket or ring will begin to wear or dry out. It should be replaced at least once a year, or more often if the pressure cooker is used more frequently.

Reason: Pressure-regulator valve is dirty and/or obstructed:
Solution: The pressure-regulator valve can become dirty when cooking. Clean the valve after each use as explained in your user's manual.

Steam is coming out from around the handle; is that normal?

A small amount of steam coming from around the handle is normal. This is one of our built in safety features that allows the pressure cooker to safely regulate the amount of pressure inside the cooker at all times.

Steam is escaping from around the edge of the lid. What is the problem?

Reason: The pressure cooker is too full.

Solution: Never fill the pressure cooker more than two-thirds full.

Reason: The pressure cooker was not closed properly.

Solution: Make sure the pressure cooker is properly closed so that a tight seal is created. Consult your user's manual for detailed instructions.

Reason: The rubber sealing gasket or ring is:

Not in place- Always check to make sure that the rubber sealing gasket or ring is inserted

Improperly positioned- Always check to see that the rubber sealing gasket or ring is properly inserted before using the pressure cooker each time

Dirty- The rubber gasket or ring should be removed from the lid and washed after each use. Refer to your instruction manual for care and maintenance tips.

Worn- After continued use, the rubber sealing gasket or ring will begin to wear or dry out. It should be replaced at least once a year, or more often if the pressure cooker is used more frequently.

The food is undercooked. What did I do wrong?

The cooking time may have been too short or the cold-water release method was incorrectly used to release pressure. Always consult the cooking times provided with the recipes. When called for in the recipe, use the slower, natural release method so that the food has the benefit of additional cooking time as the pressure drops.

The food is overcooked. What did I do wrong?

The cooking time may have been too long or the natural-release method was incorrectly used. Always consult the cooking times provided with the recipes. If the food is still overcooked, next time shorten the cooking time by at least 1 to 2 minutes. Try using the cold-water release method so that the pressure drops immediately.

INDEX